Download the New ~~In Chess~~ app:

- get early access to every issue
- follow every move on the built-in board

Read New In Chess on your tablet, smartphone or Windows PC, two weeks before the printed edition is available, and replay all the moves in the interactive chess viewer

You can now download the digital edition of New In Chess on your tablet, phone or PC/notebook and read all the stories immediately after publication. By simply tapping on the games you can replay the moves on the interactive chessviewer. So from now on you don't need a board and set to fully enjoy what top grandmasters have to say about their games! The New In Chess app installs in seconds, has all the right features and is easy to operate. We have made an entire issue available as a FREE DOWNLOAD.

The chess magazine that moves
Now available for iOS, Android and Windows

Contents

'Social media? I prefer live communication ☺'

CONTRIBUTORS TO THIS ISSUE
Maxim Dlugy, Daniil Dubov, Jan-Krzysztof Duda, Anish Giri, John Henderson, Ni Hua, Gawain Jones, Kateryna Lagno, Luke McShane, Bruce Monson, Hikaru Nakamura, Peter Heine Nielsen, Maxim Notkin, Arthur van de Oudeweetering, Judit Polgar, Natasha Regan, Matthew Sadler, Misha Savinov, Jon Speelman, Jan Timman, Ju Wenjun

Valley of the Kings

The Valley of the Kings – the burial site of King Tutankhamun – set in the ancient city of Thebes, is one of Egypt's most visited attractions. These beautiful painted tombs have been designated a World Heritage Site by UNESCO. For hundreds of years, the kings, queens and nobles of the New Kingdom (1500-1070 B.C.) were buried in the valley.

Nowadays, Cairo is where you can find the kings and queens, not to mention also the bishops, knights, rooks and pawns, with increasingly popular international chess tournaments held there such as the Golden Cleopatra Open and the Egyptian Open. It's often very hot and dusty and everyone just wants to be in the shade – but who could resist a visit to the nearby pyramids?

Certainly not photojournalist Alina l'Ami, who during the 2016 Egyptian Open, when the organizers arranged a promotional tour of the pyramids, captured the juxtaposition of kings and queens in this photograph, as Bulgarian GM Marian Petrov brought along a chess set to point out the finer points to one of his game's to international arbiter, Omar Salama, who cleverly protects himself against the sun with a hat. Both are seemingly oblivious to the historic burial site of kings and queens behind them – and to the horse-mounted gentleman who seems to be approaching the chess action at a gallop! ■

The King of Atlantis

The latest superhero movie, *Aquaman*, has defied expectations to become the highest-grossing DC Extended Universe film. In the first week of January, the James Wan-directed underwater flick has grossed $887 million worldwide, though not expected to beat the $1,085 billion made by *The Dark Knight Rises*, which centres on Batman but was not part of the DCEU comic book franchise.

Ahead of the movie's release, the leading stars were featured in profiles in the media. The character that grabbed our attention was not the King of Atlantis himself but the superhero's arch-nemesis, Black Manta, played by Yahya Abdul-Mateen II, especially as *The New York Times* profiled him partaking in his favourite past-time: chess.

Despite his onscreen bravado as a supervillain, the charismatic New Orleans actor is attracted to the quieter pursuit of chess, and was taking lessons in Union Square Park in Manhattan, with Douglas Miller, a chess teacher recommended by a friend. 'I can quiet myself and allow myself to shut up and think', as

Yahya Abdul-Mateen II relishing the silence of chess in Union Square Park.

he explained his love for the game while staring intensely at the green-and-white roll-up board and plastic Staunton set. 'I really enjoy that, I enjoy silence. I find that I need it, especially in a very loud business, one that always asks me to speak, to perform.'

After looking over his games and spotting his weaknesses, the chess teacher suggested his new student should put away the superhero comic books and start reading *My System* by Aron Nimzowitsch.

Ono, Yoko!

Being arguably the most controversial woman in rock history couldn't have been easy. While best known as the widow of John Lennon – and, for many, the reason for The Beatles' breakup – Yoko Ono has always been, first and foremost, an artist. Not only that, but an artist who has supported

Yoko and Judit: kitchen table talk about chess.

chess both through her work and with her generous financial support for the game to be taught to children.

Her support for chess has now been officially recognized. Immediately after the Carlsen-Caruana match in London, match commentator Judit Polgar made a detour to Ono's New York City home to bestow on the legendary artist the Goodwill Ambassador of Artistic Values of Chess award.

The prize was announced during Polgar's Global Chess Festival last October, and awarded for the first time to celebrate artists that have expressed the outstanding values of chess in their art. One of Ono's most famous and most provocative works on the subject was her 1966 'Play It By Trust', the chess set with only white pieces on a white board that also featured prominently in the filming for Lennon's 1971 'Imagine' album.

On receiving the award, Ono said that, thanks to Judit Polgar, the image of chess as a male-dominated sport has changed. 'By showing her talents and perseverance, she proved it is a mistake to believe that women cannot be good chess players. I thank her in the name of all the women in the world.'

Destiny

Another artist who has been inspired to include chess in her work is Tanja Swart from Lisse, the Netherlands, whose geometric body of work always seems to include some sort of chess connection in it, whether that be a chequered chessboard theme or a randomly placed chess piece.

Swart, who graduated from the Royal Academy for Visual Arts in The Hague, currently has her work featured for the first time in the influential Saatchi Art Gallery in London. And true to form, her latest oil painting on canvass in the collection, 'Destiny' – 24.8 x 16.9 x 1 inches and priced at $1,190 – comes with a big chess connection.

Describing the work on the Saatchi website, Swart says: 'I really like labyrinths or a maze. So exciting to turn corners not knowing what you will see. Looking for a way out, discovering new things, meeting others.

Tanja Swart's 'Destiny'. The position looks unclear!

It's where our life can continue when we fall off our safe chess game. But it's only then when we know how to play chess. I think it's something like looking for new spaces in life but already comfortable with the rules of chess. Like growing old...'

Chess' arrogant bad boy

What do you do after you retain the World Championship crown? Well, if your name happens to be Magnus Carlsen, you – Eminem-style – make your debut as a rapper with the tag of being chess' arrogant bad boy!

Magnus showed a new talent by teaming up with Norwegian rapper Mr. Pimp Lotion on his new single,

Mr. Pimp-Lotion looking for a real MC.

'Hvem Stjal Spenolen?', all about just who stole his moisturizer, that can be heard on Spotify. For those hard of Norwegian and rap, we've taken the trouble to organize a little translating. At 6:10 into the song, Pimp Lotion introduces Magnus:

I don't think this works, we need to change strategy.
This is just nonsense and conspiracy theory.
We need a genius, a real MC.
A mastermind who doesn't offer draw.

(Magnus): Pimp L, pour something expensive in my glass
When Carlsen enters the building, the pieces fall into place.
I'm chess' arrogant bad boy.
The board game's most relevant bad boy.

And none of the suspects are bluffing. The one who stole the moisturiser was a real duffer.

(Pimp L): Was it Kasparov? Or Fabiano?
(Magnus): A-ah, wrong again, Lotiano.
(Pimp L): Okay, was it Agdestein, mane?
(Magnus): Nope, njet, nei, the culprit is the son of a former coach.
(Pimp L): Oh holy shit, I know who you mean.
(Magnus): Check mate, Ola-Jo Semb.

This is not the first time the World Champion has been linked to a hip hop song. In 2015, American rapper The Game released a song titled 'Magnus Carlsen', without flattering other references to the Norwegian in the text.

Kid's got game!

The latest prodigy who could be on a fast-track to international chess stardom is Christopher Yoo, who last September, at the age of 11, became the youngest player in history to win the CalChess State Championship, the official championship of Northern California, held at the Berkeley Chess School.

With an unbeaten score of 5½/6, that also included a crucial win over pre-tournament favourite and multi-time champion GM Enrico Sevillano, Yoo dominated to take clear first ahead of the experienced field – and in doing so, he created a little history along the way by smashing by five years the previous record set at the age of 16 by current US Champion Sam Shankland, who on hearing the news, tweeted a congratulatory: 'Kid's got game!'

The official 'Yoo watch-list' began after that victory, with the youngster looking to hunt down his third and final International Master norm. And Yoo, who recently turned 12, started 2019 with a bang by beating top-seed Le Quang Liem in the Bay Area Inter-

Christopher Yoo, youngest-ever American IM.

national in Burlingame, California, making him the youngest player ever to defeat a super-GM (2700+) in a norm tournament. The game, which sensationally gave Yoo the tournament lead at the midpoint, turned on a speculative piece sacrifice from the youngster that led to a complicated position. And although he narrowly failed to achieve his first GM norm, Yoo did gain his third and final norm to become the youngest-ever American International Master.

Christopher Yoo
Le Quang Liem
Bay Area International 2019

position after 26.♖d1

26...♖e2? Liem had to play 26...♖f5 27.♕h8+ ♚e7 28.♖e1+ ♚d7 29.♕e8+ ♚c7 30.♖c1+ ♝c5 and the king is safe. But in going for the mate, he's overlooked that Yoo has a nasty knight fork. **27.♘h7+! ♚e7 28.♕f6+ ♚d7 29.♕xd6+! ♘xd6 30.♘f6+ ♚e6 31.♘xg4 ♖xb2 32.♘e3** And White went on to easily convert the endgame advantage (1-0, 48). ■

Your Move

Rational vs irrational

Carlsen's draw offer against Caruana in their 12th World Championship game has been criticized by Kasparov, Kramnik and many others, because Carlsen's final position was better. However, probability calculations show that Carlsen's offer was rational.

AlphaZero gave Black (Carlsen) about 60% expected score in the final position, say through 60% draws (common percentage in complex asymmetric positions between equally strong top players), 30% wins, and 10% losses. When the decision had mattered (if no draw), Carlsen's winning odds of playing on would therefore have been 30:10, i.e. 3:1.

Carlsen's Elo rating for rapid exceeded Caruana's by almost 100 points, which for one game gives almost identical probabilities as just specified. That is, one rapid game would give Carlsen similarly favourable odds as having played on in the 12th game. However, the tiebreak involved four rapid games rather than one, and this gives the stronger player a bigger chance of winning overall. Calculations give 60% gain and 13% loss probabilities, i.e. odds 60:13 = 4.5:1. There remains 27% probability at an even score 2-2, leading to blitz games. There Carlsen's Elo exceeded Caruana's by 172 points, making the remaining odds even more favourable to him. His overall probability of winning the tiebreak exceeded 80%, way more than Kramnik's estimated 60% but well consistent with the historical data that we have on Carlsen's tiebreak performances.

Because this match was a 'zero sum game,' what was good for Carlsen was bad for Caruana. Caruana should have declined Carlsen's draw offer! The very fact that Carlsen offered it, should have alarmed him. Kasparov couldn't have been more off when predicting: 'In light of this shocking draw offer from Magnus in a superior position with more time, I reconsider my evaluation of him being the favourite in rapids. Tiebreaks require tremendous nerves and he seems to be losing his.' Both probability calculus and history have proven Kasparov wrong here.

More sophisticated analysis can alter the numbers in either direction, but not the conclusion that Carlsen's draw offer was fully justifiable. If I may end with some psychology: imagine how confused Carlsen would have been had Caruana declined his offer!

Peter Wakker
Rotterdam, The Netherlands

Don't care what people think

Bruce Margolis, drawing on 60 years of experience, calls Carlsen's draw offer at move 31 in Game 12

Write to us
New In Chess, P.O. Box 1093
1810 KB Alkmaar, The Netherlands
or e-mail: editors@newinchess.com
Letters may be edited or abridged

'a disgrace'. Jim Robertson would exclude Carlsen from his list of super-greats: Lasker, Capablanca, Alekhine, Botvinnik, Tal, Fischer or Kasparov. Both have short memories.

Lasker resigned his match with Capablanca in 1921 after 14 of the projected 24 games, of which 3 games were miniature draws (25 moves or less). Super-greats resign matches halfway?

The 1927 Capablanca-Alekhine match contained four miniature draws. Alekhine scrupulously avoided a return match with Capablanca, and refused to play in tournaments where they might meet until 1936. The behaviour of a super-great?

Botvinnik, who Bruce Margolis surely remembers, never once won a match as World Champion. He retained the title by having the advantage of the draw (1951, 1954), or regained it because the champion (but not the challenger) had the right to a rematch (1957, 1960). In those far-off days, the players played a leisurely 3 games a week with an adjournment after 40 moves in a 5-hour session. In 1957, Botvinnik effectively gave up at the end, with draws in 13 and 11 moves! The 1960 Tal match, and Botvinnik did it again – the last game (21 of 24) was a 17-move draw. In 1963, Botvinnik stopped fighting 3 games from the end (games 20-22 of a projected 24). With 2 Whites in the last 3 games, he played just 41 moves in the last week of play – draws in 21, 10 and 10 moves. Super-great indeed!

Kasparov in his 1984 marathon had 16 miniature draws with Karpov – 13 moves (Game 29), 15 moves (Games 10, 38), 16 moves (Game 14), 17 moves (Game 35), 19 moves (Game 20), 20 moves (Games 8, 30, 33, 34), 21 moves (Games 5, 12, 43), 22 moves (Games 23 and 25), 23 moves (Game 17). A third of the match.

Carlsen's games with Caruana averaged 53 moves. This has been equalled but never surpassed in World Championship history – Lasker-Schlechter 1910, Botvinnik-Tal 1961 and Anand-Topalov 2010. Carlsen doesn't do miniature draws. You nearly always get your money's worth.

Now Carlsen is to be excluded from the super-greats because of one 31-move draw. Really? I just think he did what he had to do in view of match rules he didn't make.

Daniil Dubov: 'If I have learned something from Magnus it's that you don't need to care about what people think.' I agree with Magnus.

Chris Holmes
St Maur, France

Threats and opportunities

Reflecting on the 12 draws in the recent World Championship match (New In Chess 2018/8), Nigel Short's suspicion that the players felt 'the pain of defeat exceeds the joy of victory' has scientific support. In his book *Thinking Fast and Slow*, Princeton psychologist Daniel

Kahneman (winner of the 2002 Nobel Memorial Prize in Economics) explains a central finding of his research: 'When directly compared or weighted against each other, losses loom larger than gains. This asymmetry between the power of positive and negative expectations or experiences has an evolutionary history. Organisms that treat threats as more urgent than opportunities have a better chance to survive and reproduce.' Chess, being a symbolic fight to the death, seems an ideal candidate for this view of risk and reward.

Dr. Roderick Hill
Saint John, Canada

Alternative format

I read with interest Nigel Short's article in New In Chess 2018/8 on how to format the World Championship. Here is another alternative.

Twenty games, highest score wins. Classical time limits of 40/2. If tied they are declared co-champions and split the prize money evenly. Both are seeded into the next Candidate cycle.

COLOPHON

PUBLISHER: Allard Hoogland
EDITOR-IN-CHIEF:
Dirk Jan ten Geuzendam
HONORARY EDITOR: Jan Timman
CONTRIBUTING EDITOR: Anish Giri
EDITORS: Peter Boel, René Olthof
PRODUCTION: Joop de Groot
TRANSLATORS: Ken Neat, Piet Verhagen
SALES AND ADVERTISING: Remmelt Otten

PHOTOS AND ILLUSTRATIONS IN THIS ISSUE:
Alina I'Ami, Collection David DeLucia, Maria
Emelianova, Lennart Ootes, Kees Stap

COVER PHOTO: Lennart Ootes

© No part of this magazine may be reproduced,
stored in a retrieval system or transmitted in any
form or by any means, recording or otherwise,
without the prior permission of the publisher.

NEW IN CHESS
P.O. BOX 1093
1810 KB ALKMAAR
THE NETHERLANDS

PHONE: 00-31-(0)72-51 27 137
SUBSCRIPTIONS: nic@newinchess.com
EDITORS: editors@newinchess.com
ADVERTISING: otten@newinchess.com

WWW.NEWINCHESS.COM

The championship remains purely classical with rapid and blitz having their own championships.

Also, the prize fund would be reduced by 5% for each draw over five. Any monies saved by such reductions would go to FIDE for use in promoting chess.

Milton Garber
Jefferson City, Missouri, United States

Quite old

I have noticed an inaccuracy in Adhiban's analysis of the game Donchenko-Wang Hao in New in Chess 2018/8.

Alexander Donchenko
Wang Hao
Douglas 2018 (3)

position after 42...♞c3

(In the game now 43.♞e3 was played.) After 43.♔f3 the suggested variation 43...♗xf1? 44.♞xf1 ♖xf2+ 45.♔xf2 ♞xe4+ leads to a dead draw, as White holds both after 46.♔f3 ♞d6 47.♞e3 ♞f5 48.♔g2 and 48.♞g4/49.♞e5 without any problems.
Instead, Black can maintain the pressure by playing something like 43...♔g7, or even better 43...♖a3 44.♔g2 ♖a4 45.♔f3 ♞d1 46.♖h2 ♔g7, when White soon loses a pawn. Anyway, the article was quite interesting!

In the same issue Grandmaster Sadler mentions a useful recommendation to start the calculation from the most forcing moves. It can be found in the 5th book of the five-volume series by IM Dvoretsky and GM Jussupow in the very first chapter, so it is not that novel. Grand-

master Krasenkow also mentions a similar advice in the next chapter. Given that Benjamin Blumenfeld (again!) and Alexander Kotov had dealt with the problem of the calculation before, I believe that the principle might be quite old. (Sorry, I am not going to explore it now.)

Anyway, I liked the article and the fact that the above-mentioned bit of advice is not new does not make it less useful.

David Navara
Prague, Czech Republic

Wrong direction

In New In Chess 2018/8 (p. 57), Adhiban Baskaran analysed the end of the game Karjakin-Sevian from the 2018 Isle of Man Open.

It was interesting to discover that the position after 78.♞d4 is exactly the same as the position after 83.♞d4 in the game Manuel Pena-Xoel Perez, Ourense 2007. There was a very similar endgame, as Black's king also went in the wrong direction.

Manuel Pena Gomez
Mauricio Xoel Perez
Ourense 2007

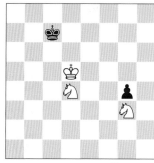

position after 83.♞d4

83...♔d7 84.♞e6 ♔e7 85.♞c5 ♔f6 86.♔e4 ♔f7 87.♔f5 ♔e7 88.♔e5 ♔f7 89.♔d6 ♔f6? 90.♞ce4+ ♔f7 91.♔d7 ♔f8 92.♞d6 ♔g7 93.♔e7 ♔g8 94.♞de4 ♔g7 95.♔e8 ♔g6 96.♔f8 ♔h6 97.♔f7 ♔h7 98.♞f5 And Black resigned. E.g.: 98...♔h8 99.♞f6 g3 100.♞h4 g2 101.♞g6 mate.

Michel de Saboulin
Sceaux, France

LENNART OOTES

He tried hard, but Magnus Carlsen didn't always succeed in escaping the autograph hunters and amateur photographers.

Double fun in St. Petersburg

Dubov and Carlsen prevail in World Rapid and Blitz

Just like last year, the World Rapid and Blitz Championships were named after King Salman of Saudi Arabia, but this time the action didn't take place in Riyadh, but in St. Petersburg. Daniil Dubov delighted the Russian fans with a brilliant victory in the Rapid part, finishing ahead of odds-on favourite Magnus Carlsen. The Norwegian showed his grit as he hit back in the Blitz, needing all his speed and determination, because Poland's Jan-Krzysztof Duda was on the rampage as well. **MISHA SAVINOV** reports.

It was only in late November that it was decided that Russia would organize the World Rapid and Blitz championships. With the dates set between Christmas and New Year, this was short notice, very short notice. But it was great news, of course. A little bit crazy, too, but if anyone can organize a world championship in a couple of weeks, it's us.

And where was the event going to be staged? Within days, the choice was narrowed down to three cities: Moscow, St. Petersburg, and Kazan. All three are populous, chess-loving and accessible. Since I live in St. Petersburg, my preference was obvious. 'There is very little chance we will choose it, though', Mark Glukhovsky, my old friend who is doing executive work for the Russian Chess Federation, told me. A few more days went by, and somehow Petersburg got the event anyway. The actual venue had not been decided yet, but there were rumours about the Expo Center – large, remote, and totally irrelevant to Petersburg. They do have Europe's largest Chinese restaurant, but that isn't much of a consolation.

I contacted Mark, who was about to come to the city to inspect possible locations, and begged to make a reasonable choice. He asked me to suggest alternatives. I told him about the Azimut Hotel and mentioned a couple of excellent exhibition halls in the historical centre – 'but they are probably already booked, it's too late and too ambitious.' Needless to say, good managers deal with ambitious undertakings on a daily basis, and the Manege Central Exhibition Hall was promptly re-booked for chess. The Azimut Hotel was selected as an accommodation option.

The Manege building is simply stunning. It seems a bit odd that famous Italian architects of the early 19th century designed riding halls. Marble, in neoclassical style,

with Doric columns and arched openings – and a stable...? Then I thought about it again. Perhaps people were as passionate about horse riding as we are about football, and there was nothing odd about famous Japanese architects designing a new football stadium for early 21st century Petersburg, right?

'Carlsen was witty at the press-conferences and wild at the board.'

Everything was sorted out quickly and smoothly. The opening ceremony, ballet dancers, the Governor's speech, side events for amateurs, live commentary, and what not. A special mention goes to the technical department: the wireless internet connection at the press centre was so powerful that I kept receiving the signal at the bus stop a good 100 m away from the building.

I am honestly struggling to think of anything that could have been added. Maybe live banter chess with Kasparov and Karpov? Or an AlphaZero stand? A chess robot

moving pieces on three boards at once? Oh wait, they had that one... The robot was busy all the time, playing 10-minute games, mostly with kids, but not limited to them. I was told Nakamura lost to it, but Rauf Mamedov flagged it. Being able to hold against the machine and then win on time is a feature that, according to the inventor, Konstantin Kosteniuk (Alexandra's father), evens the chances of humans and makes Human vs. Computer competitions great again. Needless to say, it only works in blitz and rapid chess, not classical.

There were rating restrictions to participating in the championships, but they were not overly strict. Nikolay Vlassov, 53, IM, devoted blitz warrior, and specialist of unconventional openings, barely crossed the 2500 mark for one week in September, and bingo – he could play. And play he did. And not only that: he played on Board 1 with Magnus Carlsen! They met in Round 4, both on -1, because Magnus had started the rapid tournament with a loss on time in a winning position, followed by blundering a piece in another

The Manege building in the historical centre of St. Petersburg was a perfect venue, offering plenty of space for the more than 300 participants in the World Rapid & Blitz.

The brightest young star in the Open section, 14-year-old Alireza Firouzja from Iran.

winning position. However, 15 rounds is a decent distance, and in the end Magnus finished on +6, while Nikolay had -4.

Another appealing aspect were the rising stars who used the opportunity brilliantly and made themselves noticed, for example the brightest young star of the Open Section, 14-year-old Iranian Alireza Firouzja. This young man (already a GM) tied for 6th in the rapid, and started with 6½/7 in blitz. However, losing to Magnus Carlsen in Round 8 of the blitz had dire consequences and resulted in four more losses in the next five games.

Artemiev-Firouzja
St. Petersburg Rapid 2018 (4)
position after 29.♗f2

Vladislav Artemiev had just played 29.♗f2 after more than a minute

of thinking. Can you spot a double attack in 17 seconds, like Firouzja did?

29...♗e4! Attacking the pawn on c2 and restricting the rook.

30.♗d3 g5! Neat. The game lasted for more than 30 more moves, but the outcome was never in doubt.

India's Nihal Sarin, also a grandmaster at the tender age of 14, started with a rather mediocre -1 score in the rapid, but then made a showing in the blitz, finishing in a tie for 8th-16th on +6. His opposition was somewhat less impressive because of a slow start, but he did beat former blitz champion Le Quang Liem in the course of a four-game winning streak.

Rough start

The future will probably belong to Firouzja and Nihal Sarin, but the present still belongs to Carlsen. The Norwegian was witty at the press-conferences and wild at the board. The first tournament, the rapid championship that took place during the first three days, started rough for him. He played a bit more slowly and looked a bit more irritated than usual, but he fought hard to turn the tables against both his opponents and himself.

Maybe it was the tournament situation that made Carlsen so much less approachable than the other participants. While Anand, Svidler, Aronian, Nepomniachtchi, Karjakin, Giri, Kamsky and other top players readily signed postcards and chessboards or posed for photos with numerous chess fans (more than 1,000 visitors every day) even between rounds, Magnus was staying in his personal booth. A couple of minutes before each game he would do a 60-meter run – literally! – to the restrooms, always accompanied by his father and a group of children hoping – in vain – for his attention. Then he would run back to the playing hall upstairs.

Karjakin tried to mimic this approach once, but failed miserably. Picture this: Karjakin rushes across the hall, slows down to greet someone, and a child catches him. 'I will sign after the games, as I said!' says Sergey, trying to play tough. 'Please, please, please!' 'Okay, but be quick.' He briefly looks around and signs a postcard, but before he knows it there are more children and more postcards aimed at him. 'I said I'll sign after the games! Come in two rounds!' cries Karjakin, signing every piece of paper one by one, with a hint of desperation in his voice.

Worth it

There's another amusing story involving Karjakin that happened on the third day of the rapid event. He spotted Vishy Anand in the large hall downstairs and immediately asked him: 'Vishy, Vishy, how come you did not take on g5?!' Anand looked perplexed: 'Which game are you talking about? Which round?' – 'It was the Italian, you had Black, Round 8.' – 'The only Italian I had was in Round 6.' – 'No, it must have been later than that!' – 'Trust me, I was there, sitting next to myself. And I won it anyway, so what did I miss? Hope it's worth it!'

And Sergey told him: 'It's when you played ...♕g6.'

'Magnus had started with a loss on time, followed by blundering a piece in another winning position.'

Khanin-Anand
St. Petersburg Rapid 2018 (6)
position after 26.♘g5

Vishy glanced at the board inside his head and reacted instantly: 'Right, 26...♕xg5 27.hxg5 ♗f3!, and mate. Very beautiful. Was worth it!'

Carlsen's decision

So, after a rough start, Carlsen slowly started to find his usual self. The same can be said about Nakamura, who was on just +1 after the first six rounds. The rating favourites finally met in the last round, Nakamura playing White, both half a point behind the leader, Daniil Dubov. Dubov had Black against Mamedyarov, who was also half a point below him. A blitz tie-break would ensue in case of a tie.

Dubov equalized pretty quickly and even got a slightly more pleasant position, but the game did not last. Mamedyarov's draw offer ended it on the spot.

Mamedyarov-Dubov
St. Petersburg Rapid 2018 (15)
position after 24.♗b3

Said Dubov: 'I recalled Carlsen's decision in the last game of the clas-

sical part of the London match. While he had a pleasant position with reasonable winning chances, his expectations from the tie-break were even higher, so the decision to take a draw and move on was mathematically correct. This memory made it much easier for me to take the draw. I had no doubt in my mind that Carlsen would beat Nakamura. I accepted the idea that if I wanted to win the title, I would need to defeat the boss in extra time. However, I got lucky, and he did not win.'

Let's look at some of the highlights of the rapid championship. To begin with, the new champion, Daniil Dubov, annotates two of his key games. Next, you will find fine rapid efforts by two of the main protagonists (both in rapid and blitz) in St. Petersburg, Poland's number one Jan-Krzysztof Duda, and speed ace Hikaru Nakamura.

NOTES BY
Daniil Dubov

Alireza Firouzja
Daniil Dubov
St. Petersburg Rapid 2018 (10)
King's Indian Defence, Yugoslav Variation

1.♘f3 ♘f6 2.g3 g6 3.♗g2 ♗g7 4.c4

It was surprising that all my oppo-

nents opted for this versus the Grünfeld. I tried three different lines in three games: the very ambitious 4...0-0 5.♘c3 d5 in my game against Oparin (in which I was completely outplayed), the solid ...c6/...d5 against Wang Hao and ...c5/...d6 in this game.
4...0-0 5.♘c3 c5 6.d4 d6 7.0-0 ♘c6 8.dxc5
8.d5 is probably more ambitious.
8...dxc5

A very tricky line. White still has an extra tempo in a completely symmetrical position, but suddenly all the ambitious moves lead to quite unbalanced positions. For instance, my friend Alexander Morozevich won a very nice game with Black against Anish Giri in the 2013 Grand Prix in Zug.
9.♗f4 ♘h5 10.♗g5 I consider 10.♗e3 to be the main move.
10...h6?! My notes say that Black is completely fine after 10...♗e6!.
11.♗e3 ♗e6

12.♕c1!?

We both calculated 12.♗xc5! ♕a5 13.♗e3 ♗xc4, and it feels as if White has nothing. This is not true, since 14.♘d2! ♗e6 15.♘b3 ♕b4 16.♘d5 leads to a very pleasant edge for him.
12...♔h7 13.♖d1 ♕a5

14.♘d5?!
It's actually mysterious that strong players quite often consider the same bad move to be the best. I also thought that 14.♘d5 was critical, but in the line after 14.♘e4! ♕b4, White has 15.♘xc5 ♗xb2 (15...♕xc4) 16.a3! ♗xc1 17.axb4 ♗xe3 18.♘xe6 fxe6 19.fxe3, and White is just winning. That means that Black has to do something else, but then he will be worse.
14...♖ac8 15.♘d2 b6!
Now White is a bit stuck. There is nothing to attack and the knights are slightly misplaced.
16.a3 ♕a6?

17.h3? 17.♘b4! would have been very painful. Black has to go 17...♕b7 18.♘xc6 ♖xc6, when surprisingly enough he will get some compensation and the game is not over yet. But White is obviously better, of course.
17...♖fd8 18.g4?! 18.♘b4! is still there, but now it's less effective: 18...cxb4 19.axb4 ♕b7 20.b5 ♗d5! 21.♗xd5 ♖xd5 22.cxd5 ♘d4 23.♕b1 ♘c2!, and Black is OK.

18...♗xd5! 19.♗xd5 After 19.cxd5

Black goes 19...♘d4. **19...♘f6 20.♗g2** My idea was 20.♗xf7 ♘e5 21.♗e6 ♖c6, which clearly favours Black. **20...♘d4 21.♗xd4 cxd4**
Now Black is much better, since White's king is weakened and the attack is on its way, slowly but surely.
22.♕c2 ♖c7 23.♖ac1 ♕c8
A logical manoeuvre: Black will definitely need his queen in the attack.
24.♘e4

24...♘d5 A very tempting move, and there's nothing wrong with it, but 24...♘xe4!? 25.♗xe4 e6 is also bad for White. I failed to understand it during the game. There is no way to stop ...f5. Still, my move is not worse.
25.c5 My engine came up with 25.♘g3 ♘f4 26.♗f1, but this is obviously a very bad sign for White.
25...bxc5
I didn't want to deal with a passed pawn after 25...♘f4 26.c6.

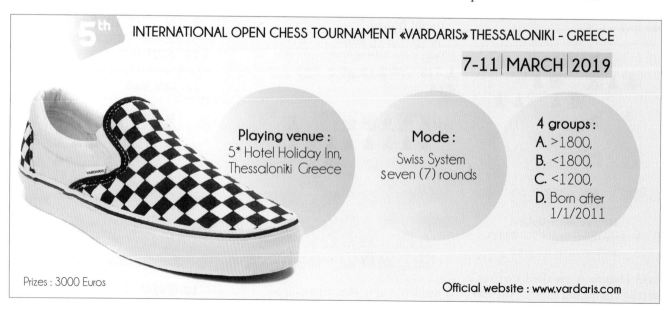

The Manege by night. Originally designed by Italian architects as a riding hall, the neoclassical building was constructed in the early 19th century.

LENNART OOTES

Now Black gets what he wants. All the rooks are on the board and I just need to triple on the d-file and play ...e5 if needed.

34.♔h2 ♖cd5 35.♖c7?! ♛b8 36.♔g3 e5 37.♖c4

37.♖dc1 exd4 38.♛f4 ♖8d7 won't work.

37...♛b5!

Coming to d7 with tempo.

38.♖b4 ♛d7

Now the pawn is lost and all White has left is with few tricks.

39.♖c1 exd4 40.♖c7 ♛e6 41.♖bb7 ♖8d7

41...d3 was also completely fine, but I wanted to keep it safe.

42.♖xa7

Or 42.♖xd7 ♖xd7 43.♖xd7 ♛xd7 44.♛d3 ♛c7+ 45.♔g2 ♛c3.

42...♖xc7 43.♖xc7 d3 44.♖c1 d2 45.♖d1 ♛e2 46.♔g1 ♖d3! 47.a4 ♛e5+ 48.♔h1 ♛e4+ 49.♛g2 ♖xh3+ 50.♔g1 ♛e2

26.♘xc5 ♘f4 27.b4

27...d3! A very important move. Black will put his bishop on d4, after which the mating attack with ...h5 will be really powerful.

28.exd3 ♗d4 29.♛d2

29...♘xg2? I saw a very pleasant position ahead of me and couldn't stop myself from going for it. Still, White

had very good drawing chances.

It was much more logical to maintain the domination with 29...e5!, which was my original intention, but 30.♘b3 ♗b6 31.d4 confused me. The brilliant engine, however, plays 31...h5 32.gxh5 ♖g8!, and the game is basically over.

30.♔xg2 ♗xc5 31.bxc5 ♖xc5 32.♛f4 ♔g7

Now Black is obviously better, and it's very unpleasant to be White, but objectively the position is much closer to a draw.

33.d4?!

White had to try 33.♖xc5! ♛xc5 34.♖c1 ♛xa3 35.♖c7, and the game would run to a drawn rook ending with an extra pawn for Black. They say such endgames are usually drawn.

33...♛b7+

And White resigned in view of 51.♖xd2 ♛e1+ 52.♛f1 ♖h1!+.

This was actually a very typical game for rapid. It looks pretty good before you actually check it.

NOTES BY
Daniil Dubov

Grigoriy Oparin
Daniil Dubov
St. Petersburg Rapid 2018 (9)
English Opening

The following game was probably the most important game of the tournament. Right after it finished, I observed that it was the only one in which I was really outplayed. This turned out to be an understatement: in fact I was outplayed at least twice. I've nothing to be proud of, but it was a very interesting game and my opponent played brilliant chess. It also proves the well-known fact that sometimes you just need to be lucky.
1.♘f3 ♘f6 2.g3 g6 3.♗g2 ♗g7 4.c4 Another game with the same opening moves. **4...0-0 5.♘c3 d5 6.cxd5 ♘xd5 7.h4!**

The main idea of his move order. 7.0-0 c5 leads to well-known lines in which Black is fine.
7...♘xc3 8.bxc3 e5
The most natural reply, but it felt as if neither of us was into the details.
9.♕c2 Allowing ...e4 with 9.h5 e4 feels over-optimistic. **9...♗f5**

Not the only move, but forcing e2-e4 felt natural to me. The only problem is that actually it was not forced.
10.e4 I thought briefly of 10.d3 e4 11.dxe4 ♗xe4 12.♕xe4 ♘xc3+ 13.♘d2 ♗xa1 14.♕xb7 ♘d7 15.♕xa8 ♕xa8 16.♗xa8 ♖xa8, and it's either completely fine for Black or slightly better for White. Anyway, I was not too worried.
10...♗g4 11.d3
Another decent option is 11.h5!?, when I kind of expected 11...♗xh5 12.♖xh5 gxh5 13.♘h4, which is definitely a cool line, but objectively speaking, only Black that can be better after 13...♕f6.
11...c5 12.♗e3 b6

13.♘h2 Again, I was mostly worried about 13.h5 ♗xh5 (13...c4!? was my intention: 14.d4 ♗xf3 15.♗xf3 exd4 16.cxd4 ♘c6!?, and Black seems to be OK in a complete mess. One logical line is 17.♖d1 ♗xd4 18.hxg6 hxg6 19.♕xc4 ♘e5 20.♗xd4 ♘xf3+, with equality) 14.♖xh5 gxh5 15.♘h4, and White gets an even better version of the sacrifice, which still doesn't mean he isn't worse. Anyway, I would probably have gone 13...c4.
13...♗e6 14.h5 ♘c6 15.hxg6

15...hxg6 Another decent option is 15...fxg6!?, but I overlooked the very nice idea of 16.♘f3 h6!, preventing ♘g5. The key line is 17.♗xh6 ♖xf3! 18.♗xg7 (18.♗xf3 ♕f8!) 18...♖xd3 19.♕xd3 ♖xd3 20.♖h8+ ♔xg7 21.♖xa8 ♖xc3, and Black can never be worse.
16.♘f3 c4!?
This looks very natural, White has spent some time for ♘h2-f3 instead of going h5 at once, and my counterplay should be in time.

17.d4! It's funny that I just missed the whole idea of d3-d4.
17...exd4 18.♘xd4 ♘e5?
The only reasonable way was 18...♘xd4 19.cxd4 b5. I was obviously scared, because it looks as if I might get mated in a few moves, but Black will be in time to create some threats with his passed pawns: 20.♖d1 ♕a5+ 21.♔f1 ♖ac8, etc., is still complex, but I didn't have a choice.
19.0-0?
A very logical move, of course, but 19.f4! ♘d3+ 20.♔f1 is almost lost for Black. Still, it's hard to imagine playing it in a rapid game instead of castling.

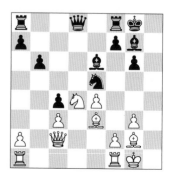

19...♗g4!?

continued on page 23

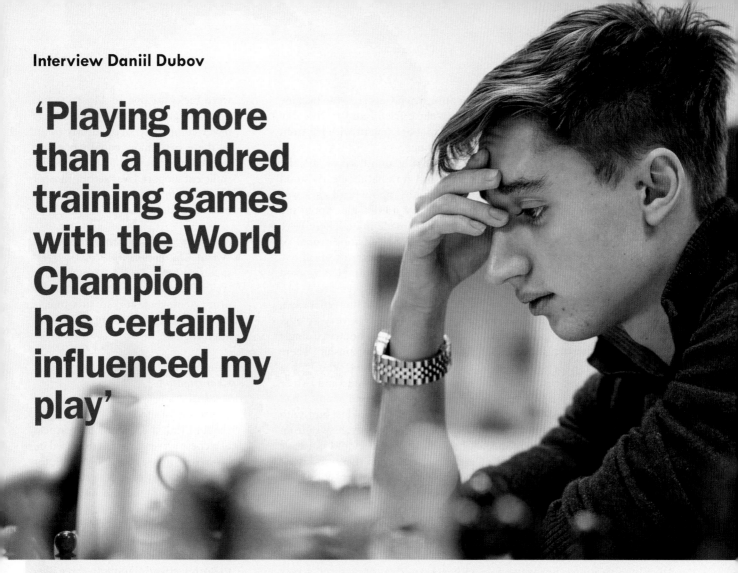

'Playing more than a hundred training games with the World Champion has certainly influenced my play'

He believes that 20 to 25 players can win the world title in rapid and blitz. This time it was him. Because he worked on Magnus Carlsen's team for the London match? **MISHA SAVINOV** talks to Rapid World Champion Daniil Dubov, who has many interesting things to say, not only about himself, but also about the Classical (and Blitz) world champ.

Daniil Dubov is 22. He became a grandmaster at the age of 14 years and 11 months. He thinks and talks very quickly, like Ian Nepomniachtchi, is fond of self-deprecating humour, like Peter Svidler, and is always ready to share his outspoken opinions, like Alexander Grischuk. His opening knowledge is known to be both deep and wide – meaning he can find new ideas on single-digit moves.

Daniil looks like a brilliant student. It would be natural to meet a guy like him in a Math Department at Princeton. Actually, his grandfather Eduard Dubov was a well-known mathematician, a member of the Moscow Mathematical Society and a strong amateur chess player and International Arbiter. He developed a formula for Soviet ratings that was more accurate than the one used by Arpad Elo. In an interview in 2017, Daniil recalled that he used to feel slightly offended when people referred to him as 'Daniil, grandson of Eduard' and dreamed to hear 'Eduard, grandfather of Daniil' some day. That day came when he became a grandmaster.

Three days before the start of the Rapid & Blitz World Championships, both of these definitions were back in the news. In a terrible tragedy, Eduard Dubov (80) froze to death on a street in Moscow under unclear circumstances. Daniil briefly considered skipping the championship, but his family convinced him to play. He barely slept the first two nights, and says the first two days of the rapid were foggy at best. He dedicated this victory to his grandfather, Eduard Dubov.

It's a topic that is impossible not to bring up when we look back on his Rapid world title. I offer him my condolences and ask him about the role of his grandfather in his chess life.

'Thank you. Frankly speaking, I would probably never have become a chess player without his influence. When I was six or seven, I saw my father and grandfather playing chess, and got interested, so they sent me to a chess school. It was my grandfather's duty to find good coaches and oversee my chess education. It is a pleasure to recall all my coaches. I started studying chess with Mikhail Grigorievich Ryvkin at a branch of the Perovo Chess School. I also studied with Nina Ivanovna Bashveyeva. Later I was promoted, so to speak, to the main branch of the Perovo School and started studying with Vassily

Vladimirovich Gagarin, who became a very close friend and to this day travels to tournaments with me from time to time.

'I probably don't know all the details, but grandfather clearly stood behind many opportunities I was given. I have no illusions about me being a self-made man. There were people with better conditions, of course, but mine were well above average, and everything has worked out well.

'It's interesting that our generation, born in 1995-96, was very strong. Suffice it to say I did not win a single Russian Junior Championship! There was Arseny Shurunov, who won a European Championship and two or three Russian Championships. I had minus-3 or minus-4 against him, with only one win. However, he was from Chelyabinsk, and they did not have enough chess action there, so I don't even know if he is still playing, and he clearly did not become a chess pro. There is Darsen Sanzhaev from Elista, who also won several Russian Championships and was beating me badly. Something did not work out with him either. I could go on and on, a very strong generation indeed! Neither I nor Vladimir Fedoseev could really compete with these people, but we

were lucky to live in Moscow and Petersburg, so our development has never completely stopped. My point is, there were many equally or more talented people, who just did not get sufficient support. I was getting most of it from my family, and for this I cannot be more grateful.'

And now you have won the Rapid World Championship. Your biggest success to date?
'Yes, of course. I don't have that many other achievements, so this one is an easy pick. Can't compare it with anything else.'

How do you rate Rapid and Blitz Championships?
'I rate them very highly, and not just due to my immodesty. I have always thought that the historical greatness of a chess player is first of all based on how close he was to challenging for the classical title, and, secondly, on his results in Rapid and Blitz Championships. For example, I consider Grischuk, who participated in the Candidates several times, once was in the Candidates Final – where he lost to Boris Gelfand – and won three Blitz World Championships, to be standing higher than Vachier-Lagrave – whom I also respect greatly – who peaked

'The computer gives answers, but it cannot ask good questions.'

above 2800 and keeps producing great results, but never played in the Candidates and had no success in speed championships. This has always been the way I saw it.'

Are you okay then with these World Championships being held every year as mass Swiss events?

'Well, I am a player, not an organizer, so for me the current format is fine. Other approaches can also be viable. I vividly remember the World Blitz Championships in Moscow, which I attended as a spectator. You can find me on many videos on YouTube. Carlsen plays Anand, for example, and there is a kid next to the board with his tongue hanging out of his mouth from excitement – that's me. Those championships were round-robins, and I liked them a lot, too. A Swiss is good because everyone can play. Getting into a round-robin could be problematic for many players, including myself.'

You have a reputation of being an opening specialist. What makes someone an opening specialist these days? A talent for working with the computer? The ability to get a fresh take on known positions?

'The latter, the ability to think in an abstract way. Working with the computer is not something I particularly excel at. I can access the cloud and run an engine, but many people can do this. I don't have a specially designed super-computer at home and I do not know any Jedi tricks for tinkering with my engines. However, I simply like chess and think about it a lot. A huge percentage of my opening ideas was discovered in planes, taxis, metro trains... When there isn't much to do, I can start thinking about a certain position, come up with an idea, get home, check it on the computer. The computer gives answers, but it cannot ask good questions. So the most effective way

of cooperating with it is by asking questions. Like, explain to me why I cannot go here? Usually the idea is crap, but from time to time it is not, and then it is immediately a big deal. When the machine does not praise an idea, but does not refute it either, it can be turned into a weapon.'

The previous Rapid & Blitz World Championship was held in Saudi Arabia. You declined to participate, a decision that was both praised and criticized.

'Perhaps I failed to communicate my thoughts properly. The only issue I had with the previous leadership of FIDE was their decision to carry out an official World Championship in a country that would not let several players in, and with an additional set of rules that would cause discomfort for some women. I have nothing against Saudi Arabia and their way of life, it is totally their own business, but World Championships must be organized where it's comfortable for everyone. Also, Israel is quite a serious force in chess. There are from three to five Israeli players in the top 100. Each of them would clearly have a shot at the medals. Depriving them of playing was ridiculous. This was my point. And I was not the only one who boycotted the event. I will not mention any names, but those are very easy to find: just look at the top of the rating list and notice who was missing. Most, if not all of them, did not come for the same reasons as I did.

'The toughest thing for me was missing the play. I didn't care about the money, but I always look forward to a good tournament, and the Rapid and Blitz Championship is a highlight of my calendar, a great feast. I'd gladly play it for free. Missing a rare tournament in my favourite game, with Magnus and nearly everyone from the top 20 there – that was a sad, sad feeling.'

You have said that 20 to 25 players could potentially become champions in rapid or blitz. Apart from some luck on the critical day, what are the requirements to get on the list?

'Clearly not rating. I wouldn't include in the list some players with blitz/rapid ratings around 2780, but would include others rated much lower. The main thing is the ability to keep cool. I would like to mention Vlad Artemiev. It is obvious that he is a unique talent. The way he played at 16-17, the way he developed – it felt as if he was going to be the next Kasparov – not for his style, but for the speed of his improvement. Then he began to slow down, like many other Russian talents of several generations – Nepomniachtchi, Khairullin, Fedoseev, Bukavshin, Oparin, me, and even younger ones like Esipenko. Being talented is fine, but you also need to work. For some reason, this understanding comes to us only after a while.

'So, Vlad is obviously a unique talent, which helps in blitz and rapid a lot more, because of the diminished influence of homework, and his biggest problem at the high level is limited experience of playing key games. He is brilliant at chess, but his ability to keep himself together and taking practical decisions needs improving.'

You disclosed that you were part of Magnus Carlsen's London team and mentioned playing many casual games with him. Could you sort of quantify what share of his natural talent and fanatical work on chess contribute to his overall success?

'Saying he works fanatically on chess is a strong over-statement. However, he told me he worked fanatically until 15 or 16, which is why he can afford to take it easy now. To me it totally makes sense. Time is precious, and the younger you are, the bigger the impact of your work. I currently work on average seven to eight hours a day. However, if I had worked three to four hours a day when I was 14 instead,

'Carlsen is not a drama queen, but a stern warrior who always fights back at you. This helps him immensely.'

I would have been better off. Unfortunately, I did not, while Magnus did. This is pure physiology, the formation of your neural network, etc. Learning a foreign language at 14 is also more efficient than at 22.

'So, Magnus does not work as much these days. However, there is chess, and there is playing chess. Playing chess is something he loves passionately. I have a reputation as a chess fanatic. I don't know many people capable of playing as much as I do. Sasha Morozevich is one of them. I remember our endless blitz matches with tea breaks, which could run up to 24 hours. Magnus also belongs to this category. He loves to play. He is the World Champion, but he rarely misses a one-minute tournament on lichess! This is just cool.

'Obviously he has a huge talent, but I feel his strongest side is his character. Or maybe the best way to say it is that he has the strongest will among the exceptionally talented, and he is the most talented among the exceptionally strong-willed. I had a chance to see it from inside and realized how much people underappreciate the role of his character. We played not only chess, but football and table tennis, too, and I saw a man who never gives up and never complains. Sometimes we played football with people we didn't know, and they would start playing it rough, tackling hard – and Carlsen would never back out! When someone from our team complained, he just said – what's the problem, you can play rough, too. He is not a drama queen, but a stern warrior who always fights back. This helps him immensely. Maybe this is the reason why he wins every tie-break in his life. I think the last one he lost was to Aronian, when Magnus was 14. He simply cannot stand losing.'

How do you expect that working with him will help you?
'Psychologically, we are alike, I think. I also have no problem fighting no matter how hard it is. The only differ-

ence is that I apply it to chess only, whereas he applies it to everything in his life. Chess-wise this experience was extremely valuable, of course. It is difficult to put into words, but playing more than a hundred training games with the World Champion has certainly influenced my play. If I have a special skill at all, it is my ability to learn from big players. I was very lucky to meet great teachers. I interacted with Dolmatov, Shipov, Morozevich, Urii Eliseev, and now Boris Gelfand, who keeps teaching me his wisdom. I got something from each one of them, and from Magnus too. Even during this championship I felt something had changed in my way of thinking at the board.

'Decision-making rationality is also my strong suit. I had some experience in card games and know how to calculate the expected value. We often joked with friends that some chess players are fighters because it's their nature, while others fight just because they are good at maths. Taking risks is easy for me when I see it is mathematically correct. Say, winning a game gives you $20,000, while a draw gives you $2,000. In this case even if you are a big underdog and have, say, 20% winning chances, playing for a win still has a higher EV. You don't need bravery for that.

'However, sometimes calculating chances is not that obvious. When Magnus took a draw in the 12th game against Caruana, my initial reaction was shock. I could not believe my eyes. It took me about three hours to really appreciate his decision. This is exactly the type of decision that makes one a World Champion. Go ahead and analyse his choices: 1) play a better position, but a very complicated and totally not technical one, against a player of similar skill, a single game only; 2) play a best-of-four match against someone you out-rate by a good 150 points. When you compare his EV in each case, the answer is obvious.

You've mentioned your card-playing experience. Did you ever feel tempted to have a career in that field?
'No, never. I still play as an amateur sometimes and have friends in the poker world. One of my very close friends, Sasha Kopasov, won an online poker tournament with $350,000 for first place. We all know about Grischuk, but many less distinguished chess players are also very successful in poker. Nikita Bodyakovsky, for example *[in 2018, Bodyakovsky won $14,563,871, which makes him the second most successful player in the world; he also has 2171 FIDE, but quit chess a long time ago – M.S.].* These two worlds are very close, but I prefer chess.'

And of chess you say to prefer blitz, but you passionately defend classical chess...
'I strongly prefer blitz to rapid, but I love classical chess, too! It's just not a pastime. You can't do classical chess for fun when you have some time available. It is difficult, more like a job. However, the joy I get from playing an excellent game in classical chess is incomparably greater. Yes, you can sometimes play a great blitz game as well, make several extraordinary moves in a row, but that would be pure luck. You wouldn't be able to explain each of these moves, back them up with variations, therefore you'll miss on the ecstasy of someone who fully understands what he is doing. Only classical chess can give me real joy. However, it is also more demanding.

'Evgeny Tomashevsky once said: the world's strongest blitz player is best in blitz, the world's strongest rapid player is best in rapid, but the world's strongest classical player is best in chess. I tend to agree. This is why I think defending classical chess is a worthy fight.' ∎

continued from page 18

Provoking f3, which basically means provoking f4 as well.

20.f3 ♗d7 21.f4 ♘g4 22.♕e2 b5

I started to feel optimistic again. My plan was pretty simple: since White's play is based on his super-powerful knight on d4, I need to chase it away. So I just need to play ...♕b6, put the rook on d8 and prepare ...b4. At some point I'll have to take on e3, but it doesn't seem to go anywhere. All right...

23.e5 ♖b8 24.♖ad1 ♕b6?

Actually, my knight on g4 is misplaced and I'll have to take on e3 anyway. Right, but I can probably wait for ♗f3...

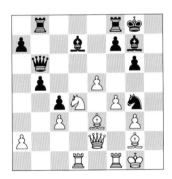

25.♗d2!

A brilliant move! That was a shock. I realized pretty quickly that I was strategically lost now, since I would never manage to chase the knight away. I was basically left with some tactical tricks.

25...♘h6

I found another route for the knight, but it didn't change much.

26.♗f3 ♘f5 27.♗e1 ♘xd4 28.cxd4

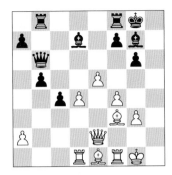

And my pawns will only cost White an exchange, while his pawns can just queen. It's also significant that I don't have a single good piece.

28...♗f5 28...c3 29.♗xc3 b4 30.♗e1 ♗b5 31.♕e4 ♗xf1 32.♔xf1 could lead to the same kind of position.

29.♗f2 ♗d3 30.♖xd3 cxd3 31.♕xd3

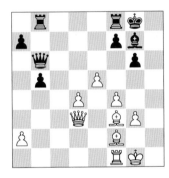

White got exactly what he wanted and is winning. Grigoriy kept playing solidly.

31...♕a5 32.♕e2

32.♗d5! could have finished the game much earlier.

32...♕a4 33.d5 ♖bc8 34.♗e4 ♖c4

Basically I should either wait for his pawns to queen or go for some stupid

David Bailey: 'I was never that interested in children. Until they can play chess, I'm not really that bothered.'
(The legendary photographer, interviewed for The Guardian's 'This much I know' column)

Dan Heisman: 'Don't be afraid of losing, be afraid of playing a game and not learning something.'
(Words of wisdom from the US chess coach)

Jeremy Hunt MP: 'Our position is very, very clear ... Individuals should not be used as pawns of diplomatic leverage [or be] used in diplomatic chess games.' *(The UK foreign secretary's warning over Paul Whelan, the British-American national arrested in early January on spying charges by Russia)*

Ken Clarke MP: 'Having another late night drinking port, reflecting on the dramatic political events of 2018 and playing chess with Dominic Grieve. After each move we are quoting Churchill to each other to muster enough courage and fight for our return to work on Monday. Bring on 2019!'
(The New Year tweet from the ex-chancellor, home secretary, current Father of the House of Commons and leading Conservative opponent of Brexit)

Leonard Barden: 'On at least one occasion [I] lost my chance of the title through trying to write and phone my report, analyse my unfinished game, and snatch a bite to eat.'
(The legendary chess columnist, explaining in an early December profile on him in The Guardian, after being 63 years in the post, how his writing job once cost him the British Championship title)

George Takei: 'If politics is a game of chess, we marched down the board and just traded a lowly pawn for a powerful queen. Congratulations, Speaker Pelosi!'
(The former Star Trek actor-turned-activist's tweet on Nancy Pelosi being elected Speaker of the House in early January)

Eduard Gufeld: 'After losing a game I play the next one better, after losing the second game I play like a lion, but after three defeats in a row anyone can beat me!'

Mikhail Bulgakov: 'On the chessboard, meanwhile, confusion reigned. Distraught, the white king was stamping about on his square and waving his arms in desperation.'
(The persecuted Soviet writer under Stalin, in his novel The Master and Margarita)

Peter Svidler: 'I claim like 1% responsibility for the current horrible situation in world chess, because I did write a short memo to Kramnik before the Kramnik-Kasparov match, "The Berlin is quite playable."' *(During the Chess24.com live coverage of the Carlsen-Caruana World Championship Match in London)*

Alexander Grischuk: 'We got a completely drawish endgame, I made some inaccuracy and he lived up to his name by playing 100 more moves! I drew and immediately deleted the app.'
(During the same broadcast, explaining what happened when he got his first smartphone, downloaded the PlayMagnus app, and challenged it on the highest level)

Flann O'Brien: 'To be chained by night in a dark pit without company of chessmen – evil destiny!'
(The Irish novelist, playwright and satirist – whose real name was Brian O'Nolan – from his acclaimed 1939 novel At Swim-Two-Birds)

Vladimir Nabokov: 'And perhaps it was precisely because she knew nothing at all about chess that chess for her was not simply a parlour game or a pleasant pastime, but a mysterious art equal to all the recognised arts.'
(In his chess-themed classic, The Luzhin Defence)

Natan Sharansky: 'When I was in the darkness of solitary confinement, I used to play chess in my head, in order to maintain sanity.'
(The chess-loving former Soviet dissident and Israeli politician)

attack. I chose the latter, but it didn't really change much.

35.♗d3 ♖c3 36.♗xb5 ♕a3 37.d6 ♖b8 38.♗c4 ♖b2!?

At least it's a nice trick, but tricks never work in a bad position.

39.d7 ♖xg3+ 40.♔h2 ♕e7!

That was my point, but it faces a very nice counterblow.

41.♔xg3 ♖xe2

42.♖d1! A very nice intermediate move.

42...♕d8 43.♗xe2 ♗f8 44.♗xa7

Now Black is lost. We were both in time-trouble, so it's not surprising that we made some mistakes. I only marked the moments where something could really change, because White had a dozen winning moves more or less all the time. Still, I have the only queen on the board and a billion checks.

44...♗e7 45.♗e3 ♕a5 46.♗c4

46.a4!, securing ♗b5, would have been much stronger: 46...g5 47.♗b5, winning.

46...♗d8 46...g5!. **47.♗b3 ♕b5 48.♔f3 ♕c6+ 49.♖d5 ♕a6 50.♖d6 ♕f1+ 51.♔e4 ♕h1+ 52.♔d3**

White played brilliantly, bringing his king closer to b2. This meant that

I would be running out of checks and the a-pawn would still run.

52...♕f1+ 53.♔c2 ♕e2+ 54.♗d2 ♕e4+ 55.♔c1 g5 56.fxg5 ♕xe5 57.♖d5 ♕e4 58.a4 ♕h1+ 59.♔b2 ♕g2 60.a5

Exactly as expected.

60...♕f2 61.♔c2 ♔f8 62.a6 ♕b6 63.♗c4 ♕c6 64.♔b3 ♕b6+ 65.♗b4+ ♔g7 66.♖f5 ♕e3+ 67.♗c3+ ♔g6 68.♖d5 ♗xg5 69.♗d3+ f5 70.♗xf5+ ♔f7 71.♗d3 ♗d8 72.♖f5+ ♔g8 73.♗c4+ ♔h7

74.♖h5+ 74.♗f7 ♕b6+ 75.♔c2 would have forced me to resign immediately, but it doesn't really matter.

74...♔g6 75.♖e5 ♕b6+ 76.♗b4 ♕g1 77.♗d3+ ♔f7 78.♗c4+ ♔g6

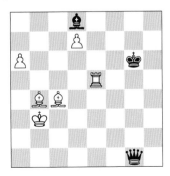

'A nice trick, but tricks never work in a bad position.'

79.♖e1? A blunder at the end of a brilliant game. Now Black captures d7. Winning was 79.♖e6+.

79...♕g3+ 80.♔a4

The pawn drops after 80.♔c2 ♕c7 81.♖e6+ ♔f5 82.♔b3 ♕xd7.

80...♕c7 81.♔b5? White should have given up the pawn with 81.♔b3 ♕xd7, which is obviously a great achievement for Black. I feel like it should be closer to a draw, but White keeps very decent winning chances.

81...♕c2+ 82.♔a3 ♗f6!

Suddenly Black has managed to activate his bishop and White has to allow a perpetual.

83.♖e2 ♕c1+ 84.♔b3 ♕d1+ 85.♔a3 ♕c1+ 86.♔b3 ♕d1+ 87.♔a3 Draw.

Even right after the game I had the feeling that Grigoriy played a brilliant game and that I didn't need to feel really ashamed about being outplayed. That feeling increased after checking the key moments of the game.

It's also funny that we were going to St. Petersburg on the same train and coincidentally were given adjacent seats. While I was analysing some stupid lines with my pocket chess, the guy was actually studying Chinese. I always knew that there had to be a connection between your general intellectual skills and your chess, and this proved it once again.

NOTES BY
Jan-Krzysztof Duda

Jan-Krzysztof Duda
Peter Svidler
St. Petersburg Rapid 2018 (15)
English Opening, Four Knights Variation

Before this game I was aware that if I won, I would be in for a nice bit of money. On the other hand, my last games had mostly been well below my normal level, and my opponent was none other than Peter Svidler himself, so I decided to keep it safe, and perhaps try to capitalize later on.
1.c4 e5 2.♘c3 ♘c6 3.♘f3 ♘f6 4.e3
No, no, no, no mainstream lines in the English Game today! I had played this system three times prior to this game, and each time I got the bishop pair after the opening. That's something, I guess.
4...♗b4 5.♕c2

5...♗xc3 My opponents often go for this exchange. It has the merit that it kills the ♘d5 jump forever.
6.♕xc3 ♕e7 7.d4 ♘e4 8.♕d3 exd4 9.♘xd4 ♕b4+
I hadn't faced this move before, because both Caruana and Harikrishna castled first, and only then gave the check on b4. Svidler's move is the most direct one, but I managed to kill the position a bit ☺.
10.♗d2
The most challenging move here is 10.♔e2, of course, but I didn't remember much theory after it. Besides it would make a mess of my set-up.
10...♘xd2 11.♕xd2

11...♕e7 This move surprised me a bit, because I thought that the endgame arising after 11...♕xd2+ 12.♔xd2 d6 was pretty harmless for Black (12...♘xd4 13.exd4 is indeed somewhat better for White).
11...♕e7 was unknown to me, so I was already on my own.
12.♘xc6 bxc6 13.♕c3 0-0

14.c5 I think the plan with 12.♘xc6, with the idea of stopping ... c5/...d6, is White's only chance to give Black some minuscule problems to solve.
14...a5 15.♗d3
I could have tried to postpone this move with the idea of taking on a6 in one go, but Black also has some semi-useful moves. Grasp all, lose all, as the saying goes.
15...♗a6 16.♗xa6 ♖xa6 17.0-0

17...d5 Black can hardly play with the backward pawn on d7. Now an interesting major-piece endgame arises in which the weakness of the d6- and b2-pawns should balance each other out.
18.cxd6 cxd6 19.♖fd1 c5 20.♖d2 a4 I had expected 20...♖b8 21.♖ad1 ♖ab6, intending to get firepower to the b-file a.s.a.p.: 22.b3 ♖a8. Now Black gets the 'hook' on b3, although creating a passed a-pawn might not be that great an idea. The move Peter played is OK.

21.♕c4 I wanted to keep Black's other rook away from the b2-pawn. Now Black has to defend the a6-rook in an awkward way.
But 21.♖ad1 ♖b8 (21...♖b6 22.♕a5!) 22.♕c4 apparently leads to the same thing, since Black can't play 22...♖ab6?! 23.♕xa4 ♖xb2 24.♖xd6, with some chances for White.
21...♖fa8 22.♖ad1 ♖b6 23.g3

23...h6?! Objectively OK, but 23...g6 24.h4 h5 would have been far more practical. Black creates more luft, and any possible four against three rook ending is an easy draw with the pawn on h5.
24.h4

24...♖aa6

After this move I realized that my opponent might be suffering, because playing without a clear plan is always difficult for humans to handle.

24...♕e6! is a computer-like move, and a very strong one, I think. White is more or less forced to take a draw after 25.♕xe6 fxe6 26.♖xd6 ♖xb2 27.♖d8+ ♖xd8 28.♖xd8+ ♔f7 29.♖c8 ♖c2 30.a3, and it will be a draw.

I expected my opponent to play 24...♕f6. Now ...♖ab8 is the idea, when White can't take on d6, since this would allow Black to take on f2. I didn't see any way to reinforce the position, and after 25.♔g2 ♖ab8 26.♕xa4 ♖xb2 27.♕c6 g6 it should be a draw.

25.♖d5

Now the idea is to play ♖1d2, and perhaps e4-e5 at some point.

25...♕b7 26.♖1d2

White has a minuscule edge, but even in my wildest dreams I couldn't have thought that I would win in 10 more moves!

26...♖b4 27.♕c2

Thinking about e4-e5...

27...♕e7 28.♕d1

Interesting was 28.a3!? ♖b3 29.♕d1,

A tall order. Serbian GM Aleksandar Indjic arrives to play Jan-Krzysztof Duda (0-1 in 21 moves).

because it makes 29...♕b7 dubious for allowing a nice manoeuvre: 30.♕g4!.

28.a3 was playable, but I didn't want to make such a committal move without having to. Perhaps I would play it after a repetition of moves after 28...♕b7, as later in the game.

28...♕e4

I had the feeling that there might be something wrong with this move, but I didn't know why.

28...♕b7 was interesting, because White doesn't get anything after 29.♖xd6 ♖xd6 30.♖xd6 ♖xb2 31.♖d8+ (31.♕xa4?? ♕f3) 31...♔h7 32.♕d3+ g6 33.e4. This looks sharp, but the engine's 0.00 tells it all...

28...♖ab6 was my main concern. It looked logical to me to activate the passive rook, even though it allows a four vs three rook ending that

Peter should hold easily: 29.♖xd6 ♖xd6 30.♖xd6 ♖xb2 31.♕d5! ♕b7 32.♕xb7 ♖xb7 33.♖a6 ♖b2 34.♖xa4 h5! (the point! Black doesn't have to rush exchanging the queenside pawns. He can improve his kingside first) 35.♔g2 g6, with a drawn ending.

29.a3

In the end, I decided on this move, because the pawn on a2 was hanging in some variations.

29...♖b3 30.♕e2 ♖bb6 31.h5

Dooming my opponent to passivity...

31...♕e6

The 31...♔f8!? wait-and-see approach was called for here.

32.♕d3

Now I get control of the b1-h7 diagonal, and I'm still threatening e4-e5...

32...♕g4? 33.♔g2?

33.♖f5! was winning at once. I saw this nice idea, but decided to cover the h3-square first, and threaten f3. Needlessly so!: 33...♕h3 (33...g6 34.hxg6 ♕xg6 35.♕d5 ♔g7 36.♖f4, and White is completely winning, or 33...c4 34.♕d5 ♖a7 35.♔g2 winning, or 33...♖a7 34.♔g2) 34.♕e4 ♖a7 (34...♖b8 35.♖xf7! ♔xf7 36.♕c4+) 35.♖e5!?, and White wins.

33...c4? A grave positional error. I guess my opponent had got tired of defending. 33...♕e6 was the way to go, but still with a very passive black position, and White may try to break with e4-e5, so 34.e4 f6 (the only move) 35.♕f3.

34.♕c2 ♖c6
34...♕c8 was preferable, but White is in the driver's seat after 35.♕e4 (or 35.e4!? f6 36.♕d1) 35...♖c6 36.g4!?.
35.e4

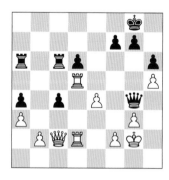

Now this is almost crushing.
35...f6 Or 35...♕c8 36.e5 ♖c5!? (36...♕b7 37.♔h2) 37.♖xd6 ♖xd6 38.exd6, winning.
35...g6 highlights how bad Black's position is: after 36.hxg6 ♕xg6 37.♖2d4 White wins the c-pawn.
36.♖f5!

And after this quiet move my opponent resigned. In fact, he could have saved his queen with 36...g5, but after 37.♖xf6 ♕xh5 38.e5 dxe5, White obviously has another quiet but crushing move: 39.♖d7!, and it's mate in five.

NOTES BY
Anish Giri

Hikaru Nakamura
Gabriel Sargissian
St. Petersburg Rapid 2018 (13)
Réti Opening

Both in the Rapid and in the Blitz, Hikaru Nakamura accelerated towards the end. Here is a nice victory by the American in one of the final rounds against a very respectable opponent.
1.♘f3 d5 2.b3

Hikaru does this quite a lot in blitz and rapid, and having lost a few games to him in this opening myself, I actually looked at this a little bit before going to St. Petersburg. Fortunately, I didn't have to play Hikaru with the black pieces and it was Gabriel Sargissian who got crushed here.
2...♘f6 3.♗b2 ♗g4 4.e3 e6 5.d3 ♗e7 6.h3 White's play is very timid, but he does win the bishop pair, for what it's worth.
6...♗xf3 7.♕xf3 0-0 8.g3 a5
Sargissian is a respected theoretician and has good opening instincts. Here he chooses a stylish move, asking White how he wants to react to the annoying a-pawn march.

9.a4 A good call. 9.a3 is no good due to the standard operation for such structures: 9...a4! 10.b4 c5.

9...♗b4+

Another stylish decision. Me likey.

10.c3 I'd go 10.♘d2 for aesthetic reasons, but Hikaru, as the Russians say, has no complexes.

10...♗d6 11.♗g2 ♘bd7 12.0-0 ♕e7 13.♕e2 c6 14.♘d2 ♖fe8 15.e4 dxe4 16.dxe4

16...♘e5??

A huge blackout of some kind. If this was played online I'd bet on a miss-click.

16...e5 would justify all Black's previous play, when indeed the b2-bishop doesn't look impressive. White should probably transfer it to d2 and consider f2-f4 at an opportune moment, or h4/♗h3. Black can also think about rearranging his pieces and perhaps about the ...b7-b5 push at some point as well; or he can simply continue his waiting game.

17.f4

Black has to be able to answer this move with ...e5!. Now White grabs space in the centre and on the kingside, and the game becomes one-way traffic.

Hikaru Nakamura pulled off strong finishes both in the Rapid and the Blitz.

17...♗c5+ 18.♔h2 ♘ed7 19.e5! ♘d5 20.♖f3 ♕f8

21.♘e4! These moves play themselves. In the end, the f5 break is going to do the job.

21...♗e7 22.c4 ♘b4

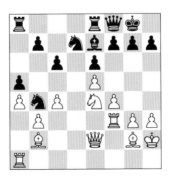

23.f5! Power play at its best. On top of all the space issues, the queen on f8 looks particularly misplaced.

23...exf5 24.♖xf5 g6

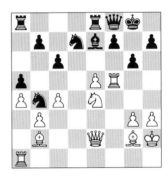

25.e6!

Hikaru goes for a flashy finish.

25...gxf5 26.exd7 ♖ed8 27.♕h5 f6 28.♕xf5 ♕f7 29.♗xf6 ♗xf6 30.♘xf6+ ♔g7 31.♖f1 ♕e7 32.♕xh7+

Black resigned. This will go down as one of Nakamura's knockouts!

St. Petersburg 2018 Rapid

					TPR
1	Daniil Dubov	RUS	2723	11	2860
2	Shakhriyar Mamedyarov	AZE	2786	10½	2846
3	Hikaru Nakamura	USA	2844	10½	2833
4	Vladislav Artemiev	RUS	2812	10½	2828
5	Magnus Carlsen	NOR	2903	10½	2779
6	Alireza Firouzja	IRI	2412	10	2848
7	Yu Yangyi	CHN	2758	10	2820
8	Anish Giri	NED	2739	10	2815
9	Sergey Karjakin	RUS	2774	10	2794
10	Tigran Petrosian	ARM	2676	10	2791
11	Anton Korobov	UKR	2740	10	2780
12	Maxim Matlakov	RUS	2690	10	2765
13	Jan-Krzysztof Duda	POL	2683	10	2759
14	David Anton	ESP	2708	10	2750
15	Alexander Grischuk	RUS	2732	10	2746
16	Dmitry Jakovenko	RUS	2731	10	2731
17	Pavel Ponkratov	RUS	2650	10	2679
18	Dmitry Andreikin	RUS	2725	9½	2801
19	Wang Hao	CHN	2782	9½	2772
20	Alexander Zubov	UKR	2681	9½	2770
21	Grigoriy Oparin	RUS	2701	9½	2764
22	Gata Kamsky	USA	2757	9½	2745
23	Vishy Anand	IND	2723	9½	2741
24	Kirill Alekseenko	RUS	2635	9½	2712
25	Daniel Fridman	GER	2677	9½	2707
26	Baadur Jobava	GEO	2718	9½	2679
27	Ivan Cheparinov	GEO	2697	9½	2676
28	Igor Kovalenko	LAT	2665	9½	2564
29	Ian Nepomniachtchi	RUS	2771	9	2775
30	Boris Gelfand	ISR	2715	9	2746
31	Gabriel Sargissian	ARM	2674	9	2720
32	Alexei Shirov	ESP	2674	9	2710
33	Saleh Salem	UAE	2682	9	2708
34	Aleksandr Rakhmanov	RUS	2613	9	2704
35	Evgeny Alekseev	RUS	2650	9	2704
36	Peter Svidler	RUS	2753	9	2703
37	Gadir Guseinov	AZE	2732	9	2702
38	Ivan Saric	CRO	2661	9	2699
39	Boris Savchenko	RUS	2660	9	2687
40	Ernesto Inarkiev	RUS	2624	9	2680

206 players, 15 rounds

Full beast mode

Having missed the first title, Magnus Carlsen was not in the mood to let the Blitz title, which was contested on Days 4 and 5, slip by. The rhythm of blitz – especially the much shorter breaks between games – was perfect for Carlsen. This energetic man wanted to play chess, as many games as he could, and as intensely as possible. Opponents were cracking under his pressure one by one, espe-

cially on the second day, when Magnus became an irresistible force. 'Full beast mode', I called it. 'Indeed, very close to it,' agreed Carlsen upon hearing the description. He looked very satisfied with the energy of his play.

Curiously, a routine win against Jan-Krzysztof Duda in Round 7 turned out to be the key game of the championship. In the other 20 games that they played, Carlsen scored 16 points, while Duda collected 16½! The young talent from Poland had proved his blitz mastery online by successively beating Karjakin and Grischuk in the chess.com knock-out championship, only to be stopped by Wesley So. It remained to be seen how Duda would handle the chess pieces without a mouse. Well, he came, handled them well and almost conquered, giving Carlsen a very good run for his money and finishing in second place, well above the rest.

Blitz demi-god Nakamura came third, 2½ points behind Carlsen and 2 points behind Duda. Hikaru was not in top form, but as a true actor he gained inspiration and energy from the crowd, which probably made the difference towards the end. Peter Svidler was having a very good tournament, but an unnecessary loss to Karjakin in the last round deprived the local favourite of a medal. He was also one move away from inflicting the only defeat upon Magnus Carlsen.

Carlsen-Svidler
St. Petersburg Blitz 2018 (10)
position after 30...♖xb3

Here Magnus played **31.♕f5,** with various threats, and then immediately

noticed the refutation: 31...♖xg3!. However, Peter reacted in a more defensive manner with **31...♖b1,** got into a worse position and soon blundered a forced mate.

The four-way tie for fourth place included Svidler, Aronian, Nepomniachtchi and Karjakin. Aronian had had a very rough rapid event, scoring just 50% thanks to a win in the last round, but came back strong in the blitz. Nepomniachtchi also struck

'In the other 20 games that they played, Carlsen scored 16 points, while Duda collected 16½!'

back in the blitz. However, an unfortunate incident in the penultimate round muddled the overall picture a bit.

Between rounds, Ian, who had no personal booth, relaxed in the media room with his coach and friend Vladimir Potkin. As soon as the pairings came up online, they would get up and go upstairs. However, something went wrong in Round 20, and when Ian approached his board and shook hands with Magnus Carlsen, he had only slightly more than a minute left on the clock! Ian made 13 routine moves in the Chelyabinsk Sicilian and offered a draw, which Magnus accepted – being a gentleman, unwilling to exploit the situation. Knowing Ian, I can tell how unhappy he was throwing away an opportunity to play the World Champion. Magnus is also a fighter, so this was a compromise that both of them hated – but it was probably the right thing to do. By the way, Magnus had even asked the arbiter not to start his opponent's clock.

High time for some blitz! Here comes a fine selection and you can warm up – just like he did himself on Day 2 of the blitz – with two crushing wins from Blitz World Champ Magnus Carlsen.

NOTES BY
Peter Heine Nielsen

Magnus Carlsen
Anish Giri
St. Petersburg Blitz 2018 (13)
English Opening, Four Knights Variation

'There are many who have fantasies as to what is the best way to start the day. This is mine.' (Magnus Carlsen)
1.c4 e5 2.♘c3 ♘f6 3.♘f3 ♘c6 4.e4!?

In the London World Championship match, as well as in Giri-Carlsen in Shamkir 2018, 4.g3 was White's preferred move. Most certainly Giri had also mapped this area out at home, but to remember this during a blitz game is a different matter.
4...♗c5 The most principled move, forcing events, as otherwise Black would just have a pleasant position with control of the d4-square.
4...♗b4 is the main line, but basically any reasonable move is acceptable for Black.
5.♘xe5 ♘xe5 6.d4 ♗b4 7.dxe5 ♘xe4

8.♕f3!? 8.♕d4 is the most common move here, but White wants to reserve his options of putting his queen on g4 or on g3 when he attacks the g7-pawn.
8...♘xc3 9.bxc3 ♗e7
With the queen on d4, this would be the correct move, as played by Caruana, but here the small details work in White's favour.
10.♕g3!

10...g6 Again similar to Caruana's approach, but since ...d6 does not threaten White's queen now, the difference is a full tempo. 10...0-0 11.♗h6 g6 might be a decent exchange sac, but 12.h4! leaves White with a huge attack.
11.♗h6 d6 12.♗e2 ♗e6 13.♖d1 ♕d7 14.exd6 cxd6 15.0-0 0-0-0

With a bit of good will, one could consider the structure similar to a well-known line of the 5.♘c3 Petroff, but here the floodgates are open to Black's king on the queenside, and Magnus takes immediate action.

16.♗e3 ♛a4 Since both 16...b6 or 16...♚b8 would be strongly met by 17.c5!, this is the only way to defend the pawn at a7.

17.♛f3 ♛c6 18.♛f4

Obviously, White does not exchange queens and renews the threat to the a7-pawn.

18...b6 19.a4! Exploiting the fact that 19...♛xa4 20.♖a1 ♛d7 21.c5! is a devastating blow, White now uses the a-pawn to break through to Black's vulnerable king.

19...♖d7 20.a5 bxa5 21.♖b1 ♖c7 22.c5 dxc5

23.♗f3?! With his opponent short of time, Magnus commits a mistake. 23.♗b5! would have been crushing, especially followed by 24.♛a4, when Black's queenside collapses.

Now Giri could have fought back with 23...g5!, when White suddenly lacks a good square for his queen, because 24.♛g3 would be met by

24...♛d6!. Best would be 24.♗xc6 gxf4 25.♗xf4 ♖xc6 26.♖b8+ ♚d7 27.♖xh8, but after 27...♖b6! 28.♖a8 ♖b7! Black has very decent counterplay. Giri's mind, however, may already have been at the upcoming interview, and things now went quickly.

23...♛d6? 24.♛e4

24...♖d8 But before completing this move, Black lost on time. Not that it mattered, because 25.♖b8+! wins on the spot, since Black cannot take the rook due to mate on a8, and 25...♚d7 26.♛a4+ also quickly ends the game.

His performance at the board was somewhat below par, but one has to respect Giri for using the break before the next round to give an interview to Norwegian TV channel NRK and being his usual combative self. Magnus, on the other hand, remained quiet and got himself ready for Round 14. There was still a tournament to be won.

In the first blitz game of Day 2, Magnus Carlsen ruthlessly defeated Anish Giri. 'There are many who have fantasies as to what is the best way to start the day. This is mine.'

NOTES BY
Peter Heine Nielsen

Wang Hao
Magnus Carlsen
St. Petersburg Blitz 2018 (14)
Sicilian Defence, Rossolimo Variation

Both the 2016 and 2018 World Championship matches and the 2017 and 2018 World Blitz would have looked average for a player of Magnus' calibre, were it not for the final day. Each time, at a very critical situation, the Champion delivered the performance needed, with an overwhelming total score of 21½/25, equalling 86%! Next in line in St. Petersburg was Wang Hao.

1.e4 c5 2.♘f3 ♘c6 3.♗b5 g6 4.♗xc6 dxc6 5.d3 ♗g7 6.h3

As in Game 1 of the recent World Championship match, Wang plays

the most common move, not trying to follow Caruana's thought of improving with 6.0-0 in order to avoid Black's knight manoeuvre.

6...♞f6 7.♞c3 ♞d7 8.♗e3 e5 9.♕d2 Caruana omitted this typical inclusion, but Wang follows the main line.

9...h6 10.0-0 b6!? Much less common than the standard 10...♕e7, but similar to Game 1 from London.

11.a3 ♞f8 12.b4 ♞e6 13.bxc5 f5

Due to the inclusion of ♕d2/...h6, Black is now threatening ...f4, winning a piece. His play is very ambitious, having the bishop pair and trying to seize space in the centre and on the kingside. The price is a serious lack in development and risks of a quick white counterattack.

14.exf5 gxf5 15.♕e1 The computer suggests ideas like 15.♖ae1 f4 16.♞xe5, assessing the position as equal.

15...0-0 16.♖b1

16...e4!? A good idea, but with a tactical drawback. 16...bxc5, simply regaining the pawn while keeping Black's trumps, was strong, but also somewhat unimaginative.

17.dxe4 f4

18.♖d1? Logical, but wrong. The rook served a much more important function on b1, as it made 18.cxb6! possible in view of 18...fxe3 19.b7!, regaining the piece with an edge. Black can play 18...♖f7!?, still with a messy position and decent chances, especially in a blitz game, but objectively White would be better.

18.♗c1 ♞g5 19.♕e2!? also looks interesting, exploiting the fact that 20. ♕c4+ is possible after 19...♗xc3, but the computer suggests 19...♞xh3!+ 20.gxh3 ♕d7!, with a strong attack!

18...♕e7 19.♗d4 ♞xd4 20.♞xd4 ♗a6 Both players are holding big trumps. Black has sacrificed two pawns, but he has the bishop pair and intends to win an exchange on f1. White needs to consolidate as well, because the f5-square looks inviting for his knight. Wang sees a tactical possibility, but misses Black's reply to it!

21.♞xc6? ♕xc5 22.♞d5 ♖ae8! White's idea was 22...♗xf1? 23.♞de7+ ♔h7 24.e5!, when suddenly the b1-h7 diagonal gives White a huge attack, since 24...♕xc2 can be met by 25.♖d2!. However, by controlling the e7-square, Black threatens the knight

on c6, since it is no longer indirectly defended by the fork on e7. This means that it will have to retreat, after which Black can safely take the exchange on f1.

23.♞cb4 ♗xf1 24.♔xf1

24...♕c4+ To make things even worse for White, 22...♖ae8! not only defended, but also attacked the e4-pawn.

25.♕e2 ♖xe4 26.♕xc4 ♖xc4

Black has an exchange and an easily winning endgame.

27.♔e2 a5 28.♞d3 ♖xc2+ 29.♔f3 ♖a2 30.♞xb6 ♖xa3 31.♞c4 ♖c3 32.♞xa5 ♖d8

33.♔e2 ♖d5 34.♞b7 ♗f8 35.♖d2 ♖b3 36.♞bc5 ♗xc5 White resigned.

NOTES BY
Jan-Krzysztof Duda

Ian Nepomniachtchi
Jan-Krzysztof Duda
St. Petersburg Blitz 2018 (13)
Sicilian Defence, Keres Attack

Round 13 was the first round of the second day of Blitz. As the pairings had already been announced, it was possible to prepare properly. I was paired against super-GM Ian Nepomniachtchi, probably the quickest in the field, against whom I had a terrible score of ½ out of 4.

Therefore I wanted to prepare as thoroughly as possible – which is easier said than done, however, because after getting up at my usual time of 1:00 pm I had very little time to refresh anything. Luckily, what I did check was exactly what happened in the game.

1.e4 c5 2.♘f3 d6 3.d4 cxd4 4.♘xd4 ♘f6 5.♘c3 e6 6.g4 h6 7.h4

The Keres Attack is the most direct attempt to destroy Black's position, and the only line I had a serious look at. This is why after both 7.♗g2 and 7.h3, played by Grischuk in our chess.com speed chess match and by Karjakin in Round 17 respectively, I got the same disastrous position after a couple of moves. Luckily for me, Ian entered the mainstream, and I could continue to blitz out my moves.

7...♘c6 8.♖g1 d5 9.exd5 ♘xd5 10.♘xd5 exd5 11.♗e3 ♕xh4!

Critical, and I believe Black's best bet. I had already played this against Mazé in a classical game, so I thought Nepo could have prepared something. But apparently he hadn't.

12.♕f3 12.♕e2 ♘xd4 13.♗xd4+ ♕e7 was recommended by Negi in his epic 1.e4-series. I think that Black may improve here and there. Still to be tested, however.

12.♘b5 is completely harmless. After 12...♕e7 13.♕xd5 ♗e6 14.♕e4, Black has equality after both the peaceful 14...a6 and the sharp 14...0-0-0.

12...♘xd4 13.♗xd4 ♕e7+ 14.♗e2 ♕e4

15.♕c3 15.0-0-0 is the other possibility. After 15...♕xf3 16.♗xf3 ♗e6 17.♖ge1 ♔d7!, Black should be able to keep the balance with a few precise moves.

15...♗e6 16.f3 ♕f4

I was still following my game against Mazé. Here Ian surprised me with:

'In the end I thought it made sense to play easy moves in blitz.'

17.♗b5+ After 17.♗e5 ♕a4! (found over the board and super-accurate to provoke b3, which weakens White's queenside a bit) 18.b3 ♕b4 19.♗xg7 ♖g8 20.♗d4 ♕xc3+ (20...♖c8 21.♕xb4 ♗xb4+ 22.♔f2!? ♖xc2 23.♖gc1, with compensation for the pawn) 21.♗xc3 h5 that game was drawn (Mazé-Duda, Brest 2018).

17...♗d7 I used some time deciding between the text-move and 17...♔d8. In the end I thought it made sense to play easy moves in blitz.

18.♗xd7+

18.♗e5! was clearly the move to be played. After 18...♕g5 19.♔f2!? (if 19.♗xd7+ ♔xd7 20.♖d1 ♗b4! holds the balance: 21.♕xb4 ♕e3+ 22.♔f1 ♕xf3+, with a perpetual) 19...♗xb5 20.♖ae1, I would probably have had to play the easiest move in blitz: 20...♗e7! 21.♗d6 0-0 22.♗xe7 ♕f4 23.♗xf8, to follow up with the superb and energetic 23...d4! (23...♖xf8 24.♕e5 ♕c4 25.♔g3 ♕xc2 26.♕xd5 ♗c6 is probably not quite enough, but nevertheless easy to play, which also has its merits).

18...♔xd7 Now Black gets straightforward play, and I am also a pawn up for the moment.

19.♕d3 19.♖d1 felt more natural, although after 19...♖e8+ 20.♔f1 ♗d6 the position doesn't change much, and it's the usual Sicilian mess.

19...♖e8+ 20.♔f1 a6

What can be more natural than defending the pawn and covering b5 at the same time?

21.♗f2?
Neither I nor the engine appreciates this move, mainly because it allows ...♕c4.

White should have played 21.♖d1, when the position is far from clear, and Black can choose from many decent moves. I would probably have gone for 21...♗d6 22.♕b3 ♔c8 23.♕xd5 ♖e6. The comp doesn't really care, but especially in blitz it feels easier to play with Black, thanks to his better king.

21...♕c4 22.♖d1 ♔c6 23.♔g2?
This move is a grave mistake, because it allows what I did in the game. Preferable was something like 23.b3, when Black remains a pawn up in the endgame after 23...♕xd3+ 24.♖xd3 ♗b4 25.c3 ♗d6, but it's not a trivial task to convert it.

23...♖e2! I was very tempted to exchange queens against my mighty opponent, but luckily I saw this move instead. Now there are multiple threats, e.g. ...♗c5, ...♖xc2 or ...♖xf2, and White will be doomed to defend a very bad endgame.

24.♖ge1
24.♕f5!? was the move, but objectively speaking, White is dead lost after 24...♗c5 25.♖gf1 ♖he8! 26.♕xf7 ♖8e7 27.♕g6+ ♔c7. But I still think it was good practical try. Alternatively, 24.♕xc4+ dxc4 25.♖ge1 ♖xc2 26.♖c1 ♖xc1 27.♖xc1 b5 28.b3 ♗e7! 29.bxc4 b4, looks like winning for Black.

24...♖xc2?!
Objectively not that great, but I think neither of us saw 25.♕xc2. The merciless computer shows that 24...♕xd3 25.♖xd3 ♖xc2 was more accurate.

25.♔g1
Missing 25.♕xc2! ♕xc2 26.♖c1 ♕xc1 (26...♕c4 27.♖xc4+ dxc4 28.♖e8! is the point) 27.♖xc1+ ♔d7 28.♖d1, and White unexpectedly wins the d5-pawn. Still, Black is obviously having all the fun with the extra pawn in the endgame.
After 25.♕xc4+ dxc4 26.♖e8 ♖xf2+ is the key, keeping Black's superior position.

25...♕xd3 26.♖xd3 ♗d6

Now White is two pawns down and his king is cut off from the second rank. It should be a trivial win, but in blitz you never know...

	St. Petersburg 2018 Blitz			
				TPR
1	Magnus Carlsen	NOR 2939	17	2962
2	Jan-Krzysztof Duda	POL 2694	16½	2930
3	Hikaru Nakamura	USA 2889	14½	2845
4	Levon Aronian	ARM 2858	14	2833
5	Peter Svidler	RUS 2770	14	2831
6	Ian Nepomniachtchi	RUS 2846	14	2817
7	Sergey Karjakin	RUS 2759	14	2800
8	Dmitry Andreikin	RUS 2777	13½	2799
9	Vladislav Artemiev	RUS 2825	13½	2796
10	Anish Giri	NED 2751	13½	2779
11	Sarin Nihal	IND 2506	13½	2777
12	Maxim Matlakov	RUS 2653	13½	2760
13	Shakhriyar Mamedyarov	AZE 2754	13½	2754
14	Nikita Vitiugov	RUS 2696	13½	2743
15	Daniil Dubov	RUS 2743	13½	2706
16	Vladimir Fedoseev	RUS 2750	13½	2674
17	Anton Korobov	UKR 2677	13	2743
18	Boris Gelfand	ISR 2722	13	2728
19	Aleksey Dreev	RUS 2675	13	2703
20	Ahmed Adly	EGY 2675	13	2702
21	Dmitry Jakovenko	RUS 2616	13	2700
22	Alexander Grischuk	RUS 2825	13	2699
23	Alexander Zubov	UKR 2729	13	2698
24	Sergei Zhigalko	BLR 2693	13	2696
25	Sanan Sjugirov	RUS 2748	13	2679
26	Gata Kamsky	USA 2657	13	2678
27	Ernesto Inarkiev	RUS 2674	13	2656
28	Klementy Sychev	RUS 2594	13	2656
29	Saveliy Golubov	RUS 2574	12½	2768
30	Parham Maghsoodloo	IRI 2642	12½	2754
31	Robert Hovhannisyan	ARM 2588	12½	2707
32	Rauf Mamedov	AZE 2741	12½	2691
33	Aleksandar Indjic	SRB 2643	12½	2687
34	Hrant Melkumyan	ARM 2699	12½	2643
35	Yu Yangyi	CHN 2804	12½	2640
36	Gawain Jones	ENG 2722	12½	2621
37	Francisco Vallejo	ESP 2673	12½	2615
38	Saleh Salem	UAE 2645	12½	2607
	202 players, 15 rounds			

27.♖ed1 ♖d8 28.a4 ♗e5 29.b4 f6
Everything must be defended in blitz...

30.b5+ Of course, Ian wants to create some threats, but the other side of that coin is that it opens the way for the black monarch.

30...axb5 31.axb5+ ♔xb5 32.♖b1+ ♔c6 33.♖db3
After 33.♖b6+ ♔c7 34.♖db3 ♖b8 is winning, while 34...♖a8 is even stronger.

33...d4 34.♖b6+ ♔d5 35.♖1b5+ ♔c4 36.♖b4+ ♔d3 37.♖xb7 ♖a8

38.♖b3+ ♔e2? Allows an unexpected trick, which could have made Black's task far more difficult. Easily winning was 38...♖c3!.

39.♔g2?
Of course it was not easy to spot 39.f4! with only seconds on the clock. Now Black's win is no longer that clear: 39...d3! 40.fxe5 ♖a4! (this hard move is the only winning one) 41.exf6 ♖xg4+ 42.♔h2 d2, and Black wins.
39...d3 40.♖7b4 d2 41.♖e4+ ♔d1 42.f4 ♖b2 43.♖d3

43...♔c2 Not the most precise, but very concrete, winning the exchange and simplifying the position. Super-accurate was 43...♗c7 44.♗e3 ♖d8.
44.♖xd2+ ♔xd2 45.fxe5 fxe5 46.♖xe5 ♔d3 47.♔g3 ♖b7

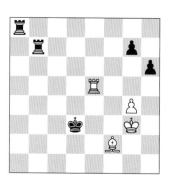

Of course such moves are played only in blitz, but I think they have certain advantages. I am protecting the crucial g7-pawn, while placing the rook on a light square, so as not to blunder it. Who minds whether you win in 10 or 20 moves?
48.♖d5+ A bit too cooperative. If I had been White here, I would probably try to pull some counterplay out of the hat with 48.♔h4 or 48.g5. Of course, this is completely winning for Black, but when you are down to seconds, many things can happen...
48...♔e4 49.♖d4+

49...♔e5! Going back to protect the g7-pawn. Now the win is trivial, even with four seconds on the clock (plus increments)...
50.♖d3 ♖ab8 51.♖e3+ ♔f6 52.♖f3+ ♔g6 53.♖f5 ♖b3+ 54.♔h4 ♖8b5 55.♖f4 ♖5b4 56.♖f5

56...♖b5 I saw the 'spectacular' 56...♖xg4+ 57.♔xg4 h5+ 58.♖xh5 ♖b4+, but decided there was no need to risk anything. Besides, I wanted to win the g4-pawn, not to exchange it ☺.
57.♖f4 ♖3b4 58.♖f3 h5 59.♖g3 ♖g5

And Ian had had enough. This was a very important win for me, as it allowed me to continue my winning streak, which grew to eight games on the trot; it was also the start of my hat-trick against 2800+ players (in blitz; in the next two rounds he also beat Artemiev and Aronian – ed.). And, finally, it put me in a good mood for the day ahead!

NOTES BY
Anish Giri

Hikaru Nakamura
Jan-Krzysztof Duda
St. Petersburg Blitz 2018 (18)
Réti Opening, Double Fianchetto

1.♘f3 ♘f6 2.b3
Hikaru faithfully sticks to his guns. Duda comes up with a creative solution to the problem.
2...b6 3.♗b2 ♗b7 4.g3 g6 5.♗g2 ♗g7

Copying your opponent's moves can save a lot of time in blitz. Surely this was one of the precious blitz tips that Maxim Dlugy has given or will give the readers in his excellent column!
6.d4 0-0 7.c4 c5 8.dxc5 bxc5

Structures like this are supposed to lead to a roughly equal game, but because it is asymmetric, both sides have something to play for. White has some potential in the centre and on the kingside due to more space and potential control over the central e4-square, while Black also has easy development and can think of a possible ...a5-a4 plan.

9.0-0 d6 10.♕c2 ♘bd7

10...♘c6 was tempting as well, with the queen potentially being attacked via b4, and then, since it is a blitz game, anything could happen.

11.♘c3 ♖b8 12.♖ab1 a6

A common idea to secure the c7-square for the queen. Just like many of such moves in blitz games, rather unnecessary and somewhat superficial, but we all make them.

13.♖fd1 ♕c7 14.♖d2 ♖fe8 15.e4 ♖bd8 16.♘d5

The Blitz aces: Jan-Krzysztof Duda (2nd), Magnus Carlsen (1st) and Hikaru Nakamura (3rd).

An interesting transformation of the pawn structure. With a pawn on d5 White can put pressure on the e7-pawn thanks to the semi-open e-file, and eventual h4-h5 ideas are bound to cause trouble in the inevitable time-scramble. Black's play has

to be connected with the ...e6 break, as ...a5-a4 looks a little slow.

16...♘xd5 17.exd5 ♘f6

The g7-bishop doesn't want to go, because in a blitz game the king would feel way too lonely.

17...♗xb2 18.♕xb2 e5 19.dxe6 ♖xe6 would be a good defensive attempt, but White is obviously slightly better thanks to the weaknesses around Black's king and the backward d6-pawn.

18.♖bd1 ♗c8 19.♗c3?

A slight blunder!

19...♘e4!

The impression I got from watching Duda's blitz games is that, for him, the game consists of two elements. The first is waiting for his opponent's blunder and the second is punishing it. Judging by his score, it seems

extremely efficient! Joking aside, he is a very promising youngster!

20.♕xe4 ♗xc3 21.♖e2 ♗f5 22.♕f4

22...e5? No need now! White gets the nasty ♘g5 move after taking on e6.

23.dxe6 ♖xe6 24.♖xe6 ♗xe6

25.♘g5! White gets all the light squares, and Black's pawn structure becomes too weak.

25...♗d4? 26.♕h4! h5 27.♘xe6 fxe6

28.♕g5! Keeping the d8-rook in check. **28...♔f7** The queen was tied to the d8-rook and couldn't come to the defence of the g6-pawn.
29.♗e4 ♖g8

30.♖d3 Exemplary play by Hikaru. The g6- and h5-pawns will fall, and then it all falls.
30...♕e7 31.♖f3+ ♔e8

31...♗f6 keeps the g6-pawn alive, but Black has literally no moves, and to be frank, his position will eventually collapse like a house of cards.
32.♗xg6+ ♔d8 33.♕xe7+ ♔xe7 34.♖f7+ ♔d8 35.♗xh5 ♖g5 36.♗e2 ♖f5 37.♖xf5 exf5

Two connected passers in an opposite-coloured bishop endgame usually win the bishop. Here White wins on auto-pilot.
38.♔g2 ♔e7 39.f4 a5 40.♗d3 ♔f6 41.h3 ♗e3 42.♔f3 ♗c1 43.g4 fxg4+ 44.hxg4 ♗d2 45.g5+ ♔e6 46.♗e4 ♗c1 47.♔g4 ♗d2 48.♗d5+ ♔e7 49.f5 ♗c3 50.f6+ ♔f8 51.♔f5

Easy! Black resigned.

NOTES BY
Anish Giri

Anish Giri
Levon Aronian
St. Petersburg Blitz 2018 (12)
Réti Opening

I wanted to let someone from my entourage annotate a blitz game of mine in which my opponent would mix up the moves on move 10 and lose without a fight, but due to a lack of those, I will just present the reader with a couple of cheap tricks that I was fortunate to find in some of my games.
1.♘f3 d5 2.g3 ♘f6 3.♗g2 ♗f5 4.c4 c6 5.♕b3 ♕b6 6.d3 e6 7.♗e3 ♕xb3 8.axb3 a6 9.♗d2 ♘bd7 10.♗c3 ♗e7 11.♘bd2 c5 12.♘e5 d4 13.♘xd7 ♘xd7 14.♗a5 ♖a7

At first I was happy to have the h1-a8 diagonal wide open for the bishop, but here I started wondering whether I was not simply strategically worse.
15...b6 is a nasty threat and once I remove the knight, Black will lock up the queenside with ...a5 and enjoy

more space in the centre, to eventually crash through with a well-prepared ...e5-e4 push 25 moves later.
I was very proud to find a cunning manoeuvre here at the end of a long and tiring day, and my equally exhausted opponent fell for my only trick.

15.♘b1!
The knight goes to a3!.
15...b6 16.♗d2 ♘e5 17.♘a3 ♖c7 18.♗f4 ♗f6 19.♘b5!

Missed by Levon. Fortunately, from here on in, the game eventually came to its logical end and I got the full point.
19...axb5 20.♖a8+ ♔e7 21.♖xh8 ♖a7 22.0-0 ♖a2 23.♗xe5 ♗xe5 24.♖b1 b4 25.h3 g5 26.♖g8 ♗g6 27.♗c6 ♔d6 28.♗b5 f5 29.♖c8 ♔e7 30.♖c6

30...f4 31.gxf4 gxf4 32.f3 ♗f5
33.♔h2 ♗f6 34.♖xb6 ♗h4
35.♖a6 ♖xa6 36.♗xa6 ♔d6
37.♗b7 e5 38.♗e4 ♗xe4 39.fxe4
♗g3+ 40.♔g2 h5 41.♖a1 ♔c6
42.♖a6+ ♔b7 43.♖h6 h4 44.♔f3
♗e1 45.♖e6

Black resigned.

Anish Giri
Ernesto Inarkiev
St. Petersburg Rapid 2018 (3)

position after 31...♔xg6

I had a very large advantage in this rapid game, but as I got extremely low on time, I decided at some point to panic my way into what looked like a drawish rook endgame. My opponent (literally) breathed a sigh of relief here, but I was very happy to show a nice final finesse that I had spotted here.

32.♖g8+!
An unexpected intermezzo. The point is that now ...♖e2 can be parried with ♖g2, and suddenly I am in control of the essential second rank. One more fun thing happened before I eventually won (obviously due to some luck, since this position is still within the drawing margin).

32...♔f5?
This is a terrible move, as now I can pick up the g4-pawn with check, but somehow I was ready for 32...♔f6, and before I knew it I captured with the rook. A peculiar oversight on both sides, which can really only happen in the rush of time-trouble.
33.♖xg4?
And this is very drawish, but in the end I was the more fortunate one.
**33...♖e1+ 34.♔h2 ♖b1 35.b4
b5 36.♖h4 ♖b2+ 37.♔g3 ♖c2
38.♖xh6 ♖xc3 39.♖h5+ ♔f6
40.♖xb5 ♖c2 41.a3 ♖c6 42.♖c5
♖a6 43.♖a5 ♖c6 44.♖xa7 ♖c3
45.♖a5 ♖d3 46.h4 ♖c3 47.h5
♖d3 48.♔g4**
Black resigned.

Ju Wenjun's dreams
The Women's section of the championship understandably drew less attention, and even the official commentators hardly ever analysed the games of the ladies. Fortunately, the ladies received enough attention from visitors (selfies, autographs, encouraging words) not to feel alienated.

Here, too, we saw emerging talents. For instance, we saw an impressive breakthrough by Leya Garifullina, a smiley 14-year-old girl from Ural. A mere Candidate Master, she chose this championship to display her unquestionable potential. She blitzed out her moves with great confidence and a shade of arrogance, a bit like Nakamura, as if holding an inferior passive position against Lagno or beating Paehtz, Harika, Stefanova or Cramling is something she does every day.

In the last round, she got Black against Ju Wenjun, and managed to draw. What a tournament for Leya! 8th place and a 2524 performance. Half an hour after making a draw with the Women's World Champion,

Leya grabbed a pen and a piece of paper and joined the other kids awaiting Carlsen's autograph session.

World Champion Ju Wenjun once again proved her dominance in the Rapid Championship. With two rounds to go, she basically secured the title. Looking at her results, it feels as if there is absolutely no variance in women's chess. Her rating is not yet reflecting her advantage over the field.

However, there was a brief moment when her rapid title was in doubt. In the last round, Ju had Black against Zhansaya Abdumalik, while Sarasadat Khademalsharieh, a full point behind the leader, had Black against Tan Zhongyi. Theoretically there could still be a tie-break between Ju and Khadem, provided we'd see two rather unlikely results. Frankly, the idea of Ju Wenjun losing a game of chess sounded ridiculous at that point, but she was totally lost by move 22.

Abdumalik-Ju Wenjun
St. Petersburg Rapid 2018 (12)
position after 21...♘e5

This mess was created from a Petroff. This is only the 22nd move, and White's position looks absolutely winning. Stockfish prefers 22.f4 – the exchange cannot be taken, because White's threats on the h-file would become lethal. After trading on d3, Black has no adequate defence against the straightforward plan:

'Ju Wenjun's rating is not yet reflecting her advantage over the field.'

fxg6, followed by f5, and the king's defence crumbles.

Zhansaya decided to sacrifice an exchange in a different way: **22.♖h4 ♗g7 23.♖xh5!? gxh5** After **24.f6 ♗f8 25.♗e4 ♖ac8 26.♗h6 ♘g6**

the position looks like a puzzle, but in fact it is not – there is no straightforward solution: White should simply play on, expecting her positional advantage to outweigh the material deficit. Zhansaya burnt some time on **27.♘f5** and after **27...d5!?** rejected the offer. The less demanding **28.♗d3** was followed by **28...♕e5 29.♗g7+ ♔xg7 30.fxg7+ ♔g8 31.♖g1 ♖c6** and White played **32.a3** along with a draw offer that would make Ju Wenjun a World Champion in rapid chess.

As a person, Ju Wenjun seems very reserved, thoughtful and unusually modest, even by Chinese standards. 'I just enjoy playing chess, I don't think about the results.' She repeats this mantra over and over again with a rather detached look. 'Do you still have a dream in chess?' I asked her after the Rapid Championship. – 'Dream? Yes, I have a dream', replied Ju after a short pause. 'I want to get my rating above 2600 and start playing in men's tournaments'. Sounds more like a short-term goal to me, but maybe chess has no room for dreams at her level.

Achieving domination in blitz was objectively harder – Ju likes to control everything on the board, something you usually can't afford in blitz. Yet, holding two titles out of three is

remarkable, and the way she earned them does not fail to convince.

Her opponent in the World Championship final in Khanty-Mansiysk, Kateryna Lagno, tied for 4th-9th in the rapid with one loss in their individual game, but was unstoppable in blitz. Kateryna went through the distance undefeated, remained in the lead for the entire event and, with victories over former and reigning classical champions Kosteniuk, Ushenina, Tan Zhongyi, and (finally!) Ju Wenjun, secured her clear first place.

We'll wind up with a game that Ju Wenjun played in the Rapid, with notes by the champion herself!

NOTES BY
Ju Wenjun

**Aleksandra Goryachkina
Ju Wenjun**
St. Petersburg Rapid 2018 (10)
Petroff Defence, Steinitz Variation

This game was played in Round 10 of the Rapid. I was leading and played Black against Goryachkina. Solid play seemed like a logical choice.
1.e4 e5 2.♘f3 ♘f6 3.d4 ♘xe4 4.♗d3 d5 5.♘xe5 ♘d7 6.0-0 ♘xe5 7.dxe5 ♘c5 8.f4 ♘xd3 9.♕xd3 g6 10.♗e3

10...c6!? A new move, protecting the d5-pawn. Previously, 10...♗e7 was played: 11.♘c3 c6 12.♘e2 0-0 13.♘g3 ♗h4 14.♗c5 ♖e8, with unclear play.
11.♘c3 b6!? Planning to put the bishop on g7 without being bothered by the white bishop going to c5.

12.♘e2 ♗g7

13.♘g3 After 13.♘d4 c5 14.♘b5 0-0 15.♘d6 ♗e6, with the idea of ...f6, Black is better. **13...0-0 14.c3 c5 15.♖ad1 ♗b7 16.♖f2** 16.b4!? was an interesting possibility for White. **16...♕c7** More to the point was 16...a5!, with a black edge. **17.♖fd2** Black is slightly better after 17.h4 f6 (or 17...♕e7 18.h5 ♕h4) 18.exf6 ♖xf6 19.h5 ♖e8.

17...a5!
After 17...♖ad8, I was worried about 18.♘e4 in view of 18...dxe4 19.♕xd8 ♖xd8 20.♖xd8+ ♗f8 21.♖1d7 ♕c6 22.f5, and White is winning. But Black is perfectly fine after 18...♗c6!.
18.♗f2 f6

Now it is time to attack.

19.exf6 ♖xf6 20.f5 ♖af8 21.fxg6 hxg6 22.♖e1 ♕c6 23.♗e3 ♖e6 24.♖ee2 d4

25.cxd4 Or 25.♗g5 ♖xe2 26.♖xe2 c4, and Black wins.

25...cxd4 26.♖c2

And not 26.♗xd4, as White will be mated: 26...♗xd4+ 27.♕xd4 ♕xg2+ 28.♖xg2 ♖e1+ 29.♘f1 ♖xf1 mate.

26...♕d5 27.♗c1 ♖fe8 28.♖xe6 ♖xe6 29.h3

29...♖c6 More direct was 29...♖e1+! 30.♔f2 ♖e3 31.♕c4 ♖e8, and this endgame should be winning for Black. But with less time you tend to do less thinking. Some moves were just played by intuition.

30.♘f1 ♖xc2 31.♕xc2 d3 32.♕f2 ♗d4

33.♘e3 33.♗e3 runs into 33...d2, and Black wins.

33...♕c6 34.♗d2 ♗xb2
Now Black is a pawn up, but White has a safe king and some initiative on the kingside.

35.♕g3 ♗d4 36.h4 ♔h7 37.♔h1 ♕d7 38.♘g4 ♗g7

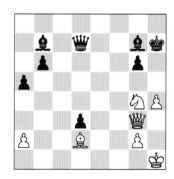

39.♕f4?
White could still hold with 39.♘f2!, with the idea of ♘h3 and ♘g5.

39...♕f5 40.♕g3 ♗c6 41.♘e3 ♕e4 42.♕f2 ♕e6 43.a3 ♕f6!

Black is winning.
44.♕xf6 Or 44.♕g3 ♕a1+ 45.♔h2 ♗e5, and game over. **44...♗xf6 45.♘c4 ♗d4 46.♔h2 ♗d5 47.♘e3 ♗e6 48.g4 ♗c5 49.a4 ♗d7 50.♔g3 ♗xa4 51.♔f4 ♗c6 52.♘c4 a4 53.♗e3 a3 54.♗xc5 bxc5**
White resigned. ∎

LENNART OOTES

The dream of Women's Rapid World Champion Ju Wenjun: 'I want to get my rating above 2600 and start playing in men's tournaments.'

The rook's pawn symphony

Last month, Steven Strogatz, professor of mathematics at Cornell, wrote in *The New York Times*: 'AlphaZero clearly displays a breed of intellect that humans have not seen before, and that we will be mulling over for a long time to come.' In their new book *Game Changer*, **MATTHEW SADLER** and **NATASHA REGAN** share this view. Here's an excerpt from their book to whet your appetite.

With unparalleled access to AlphaZero and its team of developers, the authors investigated more than 2,000 previously unpublished games and reveal the revolutionary program's thinking process. They present stunning discoveries in all areas: opening play, piece mobility, initiative, attacking techniques, long-term sacrifices and much more.
Game Changer: AlphaZero's Ground-breaking Chess Strategies and the Promise of AI, by Matthew Sadler and Natasha Regan (New In Chess 2019, 416 pages).

From an innocuous-looking position, with White's kingside untouched, AlphaZero pushes its rook's pawn to initiate a kingside offensive. Stockfish reacts a little sluggishly and allows AlphaZero to build its forces further on the kingside. When Stockfish pursues its own break on the queenside, AlphaZero pushes its queen's rook's pawn all the way to a3, tying down White's queen. By alternating threats on the kingside and queenside, AlphaZero stretches White's position beyond breaking point. An unexpected exchange sacrifice ends the game. A masterly game!

Game Themes

1. Using a rook's pawn to weaken the opponent's king's position [24...h4]
2. Opening a second front [32...g4]
3. Taking over the original front of attack [35...♖gc8]
4. Immediate piece redeployment once that goal is achieved [35...♖gc8]
5. Breaking the fortress with a sacrifice [44...♖xf4]
6. Safer king

Stockfish 8
AlphaZero
London 2018
Queen's Gambit Declined, Exchange Variation
1.d4 d5 2.c4
The last forced opening move. Both engines are now on their own.
2...e6
AlphaZero's expected score after this move is 43.2%, so it feels that White has started well. AlphaZero keeps estimating a sub 50% expected score for Black until the moment it pushes its g-pawn with 25...g5, preparing to open the kingside. Then the only way is up!

3.♘c3 ♘f6 4.cxd5 exd5 5.♗g5 ♗e7 6.e3 0-0 7.♗d3 h6 8.♗h4 c6 9.♕c2
9.♘f3 ♘e4 10.♗g3 ♗f5 11.♕c2 ♗b4 12.0-0 ♘xg3 13.hxg3 ♗xd3 14.♕xd3 ♘d7 and the world's top women's player achieved a comfortable game in Li Chao-Hou Yifan, Sharjah 2017.
9...♖e8 10.♘ge2

Stockfish plays my favourite plan, developing the knight to e2 instead of f3, preparing to castle kingside and then expand in the centre with a later f3 and e4, following the example of Botvinnik in his classic game against Keres.

10...♘bd7 11.0-0 ♘h5 12.♗xe7 ♕xe7

This is the point of playing ...h6 early! Removing the h7-pawn from the attack of the queen on c2 and the bishop on d3 frees the knight on f6 from defensive duties and allows Black to play 11...♘h5, exchanging bishops and exerting pressure on White's e3-pawn before White gets the chance to play f2-f3. If White is unable to achieve f2-f3 and e3-e4, then the knight is less well-placed on e2 than on f3.

In a blitz game against Kramnik in 2017, Nepomniachtchi tried the creative manoeuvre 13.♖ae1 ♘f8 14.♘c1 followed by ♘b3 and f3, trying to achieve his plan of central expansion nonetheless, which gave him a small edge. In this game, Stockfish feints at a central plan first but then falls back to queenside expansion and the Minority Attack.

'And we all know the danger when AlphaZero has an open file pointing at your king!'

13.♖ae1 ♘f8 14.a3 ♗d7 15.b4 ♘f6 16.♖b1 ♘e6 17.a4 a6 18.♖fe1

The position is quiet and you would expect White to have a small, safe plus. White is ready to proceed

How AlphaZero evaluates

A traditional engine evaluates a position based on a value of pawns of its main line. For example, an advantage of 1.2 pawns signifies a clearly better position for White. The limitation is that it makes no allowance for the complexity of the position. 1.2 may mean a simple advantage in an endgame or a gruesomely complicated middlegame! AlphaZero evaluates in terms of the likely game outcomes from the given position. It estimates the chances of winning and of drawing, counts one for a win and half for a draw and adds it up to give its expected score.

AlphaZero's evaluation is based on how it would expect to do against itself from the current position. It uses a weighted average of all the lines it has seen during its analysis, which lets AlphaZero take account of everything going on in the position before giving its final evaluation. We think this is what gives AlphaZero its intuitive feel for positions, allowing it to steer towards positions that are generally promising. In this article we talk about the evaluation as a percentage. An expected score of 70% for White would signify good winning chances and a definite advantage for White.

with b4-b5 while its own king looks perfectly out of harm's way. However in the next 10 moves we experience a complete transformation, and a perfect illustration of the purpose and focus with which AlphaZero mobilises its pieces. Its innovative use of the rook's pawn as a lever to create targets on an untouched and seemingly secure kingside engineers opportunities to open a file on that wing. And we all know the danger when AlphaZero has an open file pointing at your king!

18...h5

The first step: AlphaZero envisages ...h4 and ...h3, forcing g3, and then ...♘g5, targeting the weakened f3-square. Black is then ready to follow up with ...♗g4, establishing further control over the light squares. For that reason, Stockfish prefers to play h3 at once, halting the h-pawn at h4. Playing h3 now stops AlphaZero from carrying out another of its favourite manoeuvres: ...♘g4, supported by a pawn on h5, attacking f2 and h2.

19.h3 g6

A useful multi-purpose move. The typical manoeuvre ...♘g7 and ...♗f5, exchanging light-squared bishops, is now available whilst Black removes any back-rank threats by blocking the b1-h7 diagonal.

20.♖a1

A typical engine move. None of the engines are particularly wowed by

'AlphaZero manages to blend the human sense of purpose and direction with a tactical skill on a par with Stockfish's.'

the immediate 20.b5 due to 20...axb5 21.axb5 c5. Black's knight is excellently placed on e6 to support this counter-break and after 22.dxc5 ♘xc5, Black has few problems. White's pawn on b5 is now an inconvenience as it occupies the square that White would like for the knight on c3 while White's queenside dark squares lack solidity. This gives Black ample opportunities for counterplay using the knight outposts on e4 and c4 that the isolated pawn on d5 provides. So Stockfish shuffles its rooks around, waiting for a better opportunity to break. I recognise this style from my practice games against Stockfish. In these games I feel I am making progress as I slowly build up my forces while Stockfish fiddles around. I normally get reasonably far but it's a mistake to think that Stockfish's manoeuvring is without a plan. There is always a great deal of concrete calculation behind it. After one incautious move from me, Stockfish plays its desired break and my pieces turn out to be on precisely the wrong squares at that specific moment. AlphaZero manages to blend the human sense of purpose and direction with a tactical skill on a par with Stockfish's. That makes it deadly in such positions: we refer to this scenario as 'slow-burning attacks'.

20...♘g5 21.♘f4 ♘ge4

Occupying the e4 outpost and freeing the path for the g-pawn to advance against the kingside with ...g5-g4.

22.♘xe4 dxe4 23.♗c4 ♔g7 24.♖ec1

Stockfish places its rooks on b1 and c1, which are good squares when preparing the b5-break, but which are far away from the gathering storm on the kingside!

24...h4

Another typical AlphaZero move, fixing the h-pawn on h3 with ...h4 and preparing ...g5-g4.

25.♖ab1 g5 26.♘e2 ♔h6 27.♔f1 ♖g8

After this move, AlphaZero's evaluation jumps from 51.1% after 26...♔h6 to a 65.5% expected score for Black after 27...♖g8. A similar big jump to 75.5% occurs after 32...g4. AlphaZero is ready to launch its attack, and so is Stockfish... who will be faster? Well... to be honest, there's no doubt in my mind, because Stockfish's king is in the line of AlphaZero's fire!

28.b5 cxb5 29.axb5 a5

A very nice idea, turning White's b5-break – intended to provide

White with a queenside advantage by tying down Black's forces there – into a distraction for White instead! AlphaZero uses pawn activity on the queenside to disrupt the coordination of White's pieces which are then unable to oppose Black effectively on the kingside when AlphaZero's attack arrives.

30.b6 a4 31.♕a2 a3

AlphaZero has raced its other rook's pawn as far as possible into White's territory (it's got even further than the h-pawn!). The pawn is doomed in principle (White can surround it via ♖a1 and ♖c3), but while White is organising that, some big events will take place on the kingside!

32.♖c3

32.♗xf7 simply opens more lines for AlphaZero on the kingside: 32...♖g7 33.♗b3 g4 34.hxg4 ♘xg4 and the a8-rook will come to the f-file.

32...g4

The standard break we know so well.
33.hxg4 ♘xg4 34.♗f4 h3
A beautiful idea: the rook's pawns are heroes in this game!

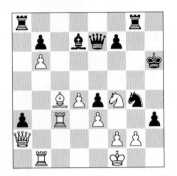

35.g3
Trying to keep the kingside as closed as possible.

A) 35.♘xh3 ♘h2+ 36.♔e2 ♖xg2 37.♘f4 ♗g4+ 38.♔e1 ♘f3+ is awful for White;

B) 35.gxh3 ♘h2+ 36.♔e2 ♖gc8 is the amazing point. It took me quite some time to appreciate what White's problems are in this position. Black intends to follow up with ...♘f3 and ...♕g5.

When you see this, you realise how constricted White is: moving the bishop from c4 is full of peril – a check along the a6-f1 diagonal from Black's light-squared bishop could be fatal – but then that means that White's rook and queen must keep defending the bishop on c4. That means the a3-pawn is going to stay alive as White cannot capture this pawn and keep protecting the bishop on c4. And if that pawn is going to stay alive, then White probably needs to leave the queen – always a terrible defender – on the a2-square to stop the pawn from moving forwards. Stockfish has ended up with its most powerful piece in an absolutely rotten position, both objectively and compared to Black's queen, which has unfettered mobility. Essentially, AlphaZero has managed to push Stockfish into a position where it can do nothing active and must simply wait for AlphaZero to find the finishing blow. And look at that

king on h6: open, and yet completely safe. Much safer in fact than White's king, which is surrounded by pawns. Wonderful judgement!

35...♖gc8
Restricting the white bishop on c4 by pinning it to the rook on c3. The rook is no longer needed on the g-file after 35.g3 so AlphaZero redeploys the now useless piece to a more active square. The file that Stockfish thought it had opened for itself now becomes the source of its greatest problems! AlphaZero is assessing its chances now as a 75.5% expected score.

36.♔g1
36.♘xh3 ♔g7 37.♘f4 ♖h8 is the stunning idea, aiming for ...♖h2. My engines give this -2.56 (completely winning for Black): 38.♔g1 ♖h2 39.♗f1 ♖xf2 40.♕d5 a2 41.♖a1 ♖b2 42.♘h5+ ♔h6 43.♘f4 ♖f6 44.♕xb7 ♖g8 is one sample line. Look at that rook mobility: AlphaZero moved its rook first to the c-file, then prepared ...♖h8 with ...♔g7 and then prepared ...♖g8 with ...♔h6! Fantastic play!

36...h2+

Look at those rooks' pawns! It's as if they are racing each other!
37.♔g2 ♔g7 38.♖cc1
I wasn't sure how Black was going to proceed after this, but AlphaZero finds an incredible way to weaken the kingside decisively. I hadn't realised how dangerous such a structure with a knight on g4 and a pawn h2 can be. I had assumed that the pawn on h2 would shield White from danger (by taking away invasion squares from Black's major pieces on the h-file) rather than create danger.

38...♖a5 An 82.0% expected score after this. **39.♗e2 ♖xc1 40.♖xc1 ♕b4** Emphasising the strength of the a-pawn: ...♕b2 is a threat.
41.♖b1 ♕d6 42.♗c4 ♕h6 43.♔h1 ♖f5

The engines are already sunk in gloom but it took me some time to understand the strength of ...♖xf4.
44.♗d5 ♖xf4 45.exf4
45.gxf4 ♕h4 46.♖f1 ♕h3 47.♕e2 ♗b5, and wins!
45...♗f5 Threatening 46...e3.
46.♖c1 46.♗xb7 e3 47.fxe3 ♗xb1 48.♕xb1 ♕h3 49.♕e1 a2 50.f5 ♘f2+ 51.♕xf2 a1♕+ 52.♕g1 hxg1♕ mate.

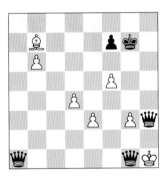

This line gives proper credit to the efforts of the rooks' pawns!
46...♕xb6 Threatening ...♕b2.
47.♕xa3 47.♕d2 ♕b2 48.♕xb2 axb2 49.♖b1 e3 50.♖xb2 exf2 51.♗g2 ♗e4 is one win, and there are plenty more!
47...♘xf2+ 48.♔xh2 ♘g4+ 49.♔g2 ♕xd4
0-1. There is no defence to all of Black's threats, starting with 50...♕f2+ and 51...♕xd5. 50.♕a2 is simply met by 50...♘e3+ and 51...♘xd5. A masterly game by AlphaZero. ∎

Exhibition from May 1920 at the Palais Royal Chess Club in Paris. The young man sitting fifth from right is Sammy's cousin, Israel Rzeszewski, who was Sammy's 'Manager' prior to Charles Azenberg taking that role a few weeks later in England.

Sammy Reshevsky
Profile of a prodigy?

He was the most famous chess 'Boy Wonder' of all time, a 'Wunderkind' whose sensational exhibitions drew massive crowds. His younger years would forever cling to him, as Sammy Reshevsky developed into a world-class player, both revered and reviled. Did he have a unique talent, a 'gift from above'? What is a prodigy to begin with? **BRUCE MONSON** takes a fresh look at the 8-time US Champion, trying to find the truth behind the myths. While he's at it, he provides compelling evidence that the 'Little Wizard' was at least two years older than his 'official' birth date...

while back I was watching a *60 Minutes* segment on Alma Deutscher, a (now) 13-year-old child prodigy in classical music. Alma started playing the piano when she was only two years old and the violin when she was three. By age six she had composed her first piano sonata and by eight a short opera. It was a remarkable story, but it was something one of her teachers had said that really struck me. When she was six he had given her some difficult assignments, fully expecting her to fail, and yet she performed them perfectly. 'It was like listening to a mid-18th century composer,' he said. 'She was a native speaker. It's her first language.'

The reference to language strongly reminded me of a comparison I had come across during my chess research. In an article, published in 1926 in the *Brooklyn Eagle*, entitled 'Lasker Explains Chess Prodigies', the former World Champion wrote: 'If a boy plays chess constantly there will come a time when he will be what we call a prodigy in chess, just as by listening to his mother tongue he finds himself suddenly able to speak it.'

When our children first learn to speak, it's almost like magic. It just happens naturally because they hear it every day. So it should come as no surprise that a child, like Alma Deutscher, who is immersed in music from an early age, would develop an understanding ('an ear') of it like any other language. And as Emanuel Lasker contends, chess should be no different.

Interestingly, there was a chess player who himself referred to chess as his primary language: 'At a chessboard I express myself in my mother tongue.' Not just any chess player, but one many regard as the greatest child prodigy in the history of chess, Samuel Reshevsky.

Samuel Reshevsky later developed into an 8-time US Champion and a contender for the World Championship, but first and foremost he will be remembered for his stunning feats at a very early age. Shmuel Rzeszewski, the 'Polish Chess Marvel' child prodigy of the early 1920s with the impossible to pronounce name (one reporter described it as something akin to 'hay fever'). The 'Boy Wonder', the 'Little Wizard', the 'Chess Wunderkind', the 'Superman' (antedating Clark Kent by nearly two decades!), who performed sensational chess exhibitions across Europe and North America that captivated the media and public to a degree generally reserved for sports figures, movie stars and carnival freak shows.

Wherever he went people showed up in the hundreds, sometimes the thousands, filling auditoriums to capacity, spilling out into the hallways and even the streets. Police

Coogan. And in fact movie stars sought *him* out! Not just any stars, but megastars like Charlie Chaplin, Douglas Fairbanks and later even Humphrey Bogart (twice)! And there were all forms of state representatives seeking his company; from the famed General von Hindenburg in Lodz during the Great War, to a veritable 'Who's Who' of royals in England and France. And America followed suit with governors, congressmen, generals, secret service agents, and even a sitting US President, Warren Harding, all seeking company with the 'Infant Prodigy'.

From coast to coast, big city and small, Sammy was marvelled at, many mistakenly thinking he was the *actual* World Champion (upstaging even Capablanca!). From Berlin to

'Police were called in to control the crowds who would break down barriers in their efforts to get a glimpse at the "Infant Miracle Man".'

were called in to control the crowds who would break down barriers in their efforts to get a glimpse at the 'Infant Miracle Man'. Women fawned over his cuteness, pawing at him for hugs, some even offering money to get a quick kiss (always denied). Children gawked, sometimes menacingly, jealous that it was not *they* receiving all this attention.

There were also protestors, concerned parents and officials admonishing the 'exploitation' of an innocent child. Even a few chess players expressed concern, fearful that the mental strain of such performances would be 'a source of danger to the immature mental equipment of the prodigy'.

Each new city, each new stop produced a new media frenzy, some on par with the receptions received by child movie stars like Shirley Temple, Mickey Rooney and Jackie

Los Angeles, psychologists analysed his mannerisms, peppered him with questions and tests; phrenologists examined the bumps and contours of his head; craniologists measured the circumference of his head, biologists diagnosed the 'chemistry of the soul' in his glands, each 'ology' searching for the secret to his mysterious powers, perhaps to the benefit of all mankind as one headline touted: 'If Scientists Can Understand How a Boy of 8, Who Cannot Read or Write, Can Beat All the Gray-Bearded Chess Experts of the World, Perhaps It Can Build Up in Him a Super-Brain Which Will Be Useful to Mankind.'

The Sammy Show
This all sounds like so much hyperbole, but it's not. That's how it actually was. In a word it was a circus; the stuff of P.T. Barnum and the Ringling Bros. Sammy turned chess into a

'The entrance was dramatized, Sammy often coming in riding the shoulders of Azenberg like the beautiful gypsy girl riding the elephant, sparking cheers and applause.'

brand much the way Harry Houdini did so for the escape artist. Not until Bobby Fischer fifty years later would the West see such a phenomenal surge in chess interest.

When we think of Sammy as a child prodigy we tend to think of him purely from the chess perspective, but that is only one aspect, perhaps not even the most significant one. Above all else he was a performer who made chess not only interesting but riveting – sometimes to the point of 'pandemonium' – for the average Jack and Jill citizen. He worked inside of a 'ring' which included a ringmaster – his 'manager and translator' Charles Azenberg – who directed the show with select commentary and anecdotes throughout the performance, much the way a circus ringmaster directs your attention to the high-wire. Even the entrance into the ring was dramatized, Sammy often coming in riding the shoulders of Azenberg like the beautiful gypsy girl riding the elephant, sparking cheers and applause and anticipation for the acts ahead. This would sometimes be followed by Sammy performing one or two operatic songs acapella, since he was said to possess an excellent singing voice. And as the cameras flashed Sammy would strike poses. As Herman Helms reported in *American Chess Bulletin*, Sammy was 'one of the best posers in the business, and with but little training would make a first-class screen artist.'

He was also armed with an array of witty quips and banter he likely picked up in the smoke-filled chess clubs and cafes of Eastern Europe where his father had brought him almost daily, the places where Sammy

had mastered his craft. 'Where did I go wrong?' asked one of Sammy's victims. 'Already your first move was a mistake!' was the response. When Sammy came to another board, the man, seeing his predicament, lamented 'What should I do now?', to which Sammy replied, 'Go home!' He even interacted with the audience, which typically included a large proportion of women, some of whom could not contain their enthusiasm: 'Isn't he the darling?' 'Did you see that baby?' 'Isn't he the cutest ever?' Once when a woman asked if she could give him a kiss, Sammy retorted, 'No, but you can kiss my manager!'

Such good-natured humour always played well with the audiences, garnering laughter and applause. Even his mannerisms played a part.

During the initial stages of an exhibition Sammy moved so quickly it had an electrifying effect on both the audience and especially the players. 'He moved from board to board with almost unbelievable rapidity', said one observer. 'He fairly ran from one board to the next', said another. Not only did this keep the audience engaged, but it was a very effective strategy for rattling his opponents, who often made mistakes simply because of the pressure of having to move the moment Sammy returned to their boards.

Once the games got into the meat and potatoes stage the pace slowed a bit, but the banter did not. He frequently made comments to his opponents, such as if they were playing too slowly ('Come on, mister, move!'), or if they were giving him problems; or especially if he was playing (gasp) a woman, or worse, another child! One example bears repeating.

On the England leg of Sammy's tour in 1920 he played an exhibition at the famous chess club, The Gambit Café, owned by England's

Sammy's final performance in Paris at the Hotel Majestic on July 1, 1920, organized by Princess George (nee Marie Bonaparte) of Greece and Denmark.

COLLECTION DAVID DELUCIA

premiere female player, Edith Price. Naturally, Miss Price wanted to test her mettle against him, but Sammy refused. After some imploring he finally agreed, but he refused to shake her hand (against his religion, was the explanation) and 'she *must* play quickly'. According to Brian Harley, who witnessed the encounter, 'Every now and again he utters a remark in his little sharp tones.' 'I'm going to show her... quick! ... she makes tricks!' 'Ah! All right!' 'No good!' Harley further notes that after winning a pawn a 'malicious smile' came over Sammy's face and he retorts 'in a blood-curdling chuckle, "She is not now so quick..."' Soon thereafter the 'terrible infant' asks, 'What is English for dead?'

The Mozart of chess?

Inevitably, the chatter began to take on surreal tones, about Sammy being 'the greatest chess player of his age that the world ever knew', a 'transcendent genius'. John F. Barry, the chess editor of the *Boston Transcript*, even compared him to Mozart, noting how Reshevsky 'has the necessary combination of faculties most people do not possess, just as Mozart, the musical genius, had at about the same age.'

Ah yes, Mozart, the gold-standard of child prodigies by which all others shall be judged. Then, as now, child prodigies were a dime a dozen. An article on child prodigies in the *New York Tribune* from April 3, 1921, observed that the number brought to public attention 'in just the last year is so great that it would be almost impossible to call the roll without leaving out several of them.' And shortly after Reshevsky's arrival in New York, the Jewish Cantor and

From the Austrian newspaper *Das Interessante Blatt* (The Interesting Paper) 1917. Opponent unknown. The photo appears staged, like others taken around the same time following Sammy's 'discovery' by Akiba Rubinstein in 1917.

chess fan Joseph Rosenblatt hosted a 'Prodigy Party' at his home featuring no less than 40 (Jewish) child prodigies in the area, with Sammy – or 'Schmulke' as he was then called in Jewish company – prominently on display along with a throng of virtuosos long forgotten by history.

While far rarer than in music, chess has had many 'Mozarts'. A list by chess historian Edward Winter includes Paul Morphy, Emanuel Lasker, Mikhail Tal, Boris Spassky and Bobby Fischer (Fischer also got a Beethoven nod). Even Anatoly Karpov made someone's list at some point, though strangely Capablanca did not, at least not during his lifetime. Magnus Carlsen is the latest inductee. He was even featured on *60 Minutes* in 2012 as the 'Mozart of Chess'.

But what does that even mean? Wolfgang Amadeus Mozart, the 'Miracle of Salzburg', has an almost god-like aura around him. The victory of nature over nurture. It's just assumed that his musical genius

was something beyond mere human capacity, explained only as a 'gift from God'. Or, as Salieri puts it in Milos Forman's hit movie *Amadeus* (1984), 'taking dictation from God'.

The truth is more organic, and frankly more satisfying in my opinion. What *is* known is that Mozart was the product of a domineering father, Leopold, who was himself an accomplished composer, teacher and author of a popular book on violin instruction. He started his son at the age of three (!) on a rigorous and systematic regimen of training, along with his older sister, Nannerl, who some scholars believe was even *more* talented than Wolfgang! Hours and hours of training. Focused and deliberate. Every day. For years! And even *then* Mozart's first masterpiece (Piano Concerto No.9) was not composed until he was twenty-one. The myth that Mozart's manuscripts show no corrections, that he was just recording symphonies already complete in his head, have long been debunked, along with a slew of other myths about him. As *The New Yorker's* music critic, Alex Ross, noted, 'Mozart became Mozart by working furiously hard.'

Refreshingly, that is also true of each name on our Mozart Chess

The man, seeing his predicament, lamented 'What should I do now?', to which Sammy replied, 'Go home!'

Team. And that *also* includes Sammy Reshevsky! In fact, when you factor in the domineering father and son traveling circus aspect of performing before the courts of Europe, Reshevsky is probably the only chess player who mimics the *actual* life of Mozart.

The Polgar sisters

One name not listed on our 'Mozart of chess' list is Judit Polgar, though she should be. The Polgar sisters hold a special place in not only chess history, but also in hard objective science! They were all raised in an environment specifically engineered to produce chess geniuses. In particular Judit, who, being the youngest, benefitted from an improved system of training that her older sisters Susan and Sofia had worked the bugs out of.

According to their father, Laszlo Polgar, an educational psychologist from Hungary, it was nurture, not nature that created the genius. He even wrote a book on it, *Bring up Genius,* and then set out to prove his theory with his daughters. They

Hollywood 1921. Sammy Reshevsky with film legend Charlie Chaplin.

every top level grandmaster required at least ten years of 'intensive study' to reach the top ranks. Even Bobby Fischer didn't get a free lunch.

The premise was later applied to other areas such as math, science, tennis, swimming and literature, and

a person becomes involved in an activity may matter...'

For this article we asked Judit Polgar if she believed prodigies exist. 'I don't think they are born. Generally speaking it is their circumstances, what kind of environment they grow up in. And how passionate and dedicated they are to their specific field. Whether it is because they are influenced by their parents, as in my case, or other circumstances bring them on that line, it will still require a hell of a lot of work. I don't think you can make "genius" kind of results without being passionate about it. When you are passionate you don't feel the *pain* of the work as much because you are so engaged in it.'

'Observers were even alarmed when they saw him: "His eyes in those little lashes seemed blank and dead".'

were all home-schooled. And while they learned all subjects and passed all required exams, from an early age on their day was primarily devoted to chess, for years on end. The results were stunning and not only confirmed Laszlo's theory, but exceeded it.

What the Polgar experiment confirmed was what numerous other studies have shown since, including a famous study on chess players by Nobel Laureate Herbert Simon and William Chase that identified the phenomenon known as 'the ten-year rule' (or 10,000-hour-rule, as Malcolm Gladwell later branded it in his 2008 book, *Outliers*), based on their observation that, almost without exception,

as Geoff Colvin noted in *Talent is Overrated,* 'no one, not even the most "talented" performers, became great without at least ten years of very hard preparation.'

Not all researchers agree. A study by psychologist Brooke Macnamara in 2014 found that 'practice time' explained 'only 20 to 25 percent' of performance differences in chess, music, and sports. 'There is no doubt that deliberate practice is important ... It is just less important than has been argued', Macnamara said. 'For scientists, the important question now is, what else matters?' One further finding from Macnamara's team was that 'the age at which

And did she feel that Reshevsky must have also had special encouragement or a special environment? 'I'm pretty sure that everybody who reaches very high must have had the circumstances that allowed them to achieve that level. And we can also talk about luck. And by luck I mean timing. If it was the right moment, right time, right place and somehow the engine starts working inside of you. Of course there is also character, how much you *want* success.'

Rage to master

This wanting success, this passion, is what psychologist Ellen Winner calls the 'rage to master'. With prodigies, she said 'the rage to master is extreme, they are attracted to a subject early and learn rapidly, approaching it with unshakable concentration.'

I believe it also explains much about Sammy Reshevsky. If there is one thing that stands out about him above all else, it is the 'unshakable concentration' that came over him whenever he was in front of a chessboard. His manager, Charles Azenberg, often said he was different while playing, 'It's like he is a completely different person'. And observers watching were sometimes even alarmed when they saw him, one describing him with a sense of horror: 'His eyes in those little lashes seemed blank and dead.'

Even so, does this explain how a boy of eight was advanced to a level we typically do not see until several years later? Historically, this seems to be around the age of 11 or 12 when there is a sudden surge in strength, most likely coinciding with hormonal changes.

For many years I thought Reshevsky was different than all the rest. Even knowing the science I somehow hung onto the idea that he was the exception that *disproved* the rule. Didn't Reshevsky always say that he played chess 'by intuition' alone; that he 'never studied the game'; that chess was, for him, 'a natural function, like breathing'; that the correct moves in a game 'required no conscious thought'; that he learned the game 'at age four' simply by 'watching his father play' and within months was 'beyond the skills of everyone in his village'? Where is the 'deliberate practice' in that? And how does the 'ten-year-rule' apply to an eight-year-old?

It turns out much of what we've come to accept as fact about Reshevsky is simply not true, or at least not the *whole* truth. Like Mozart, there appears to be a fair amount of mythology woven into the fabric.

Reshevsky was notoriously protective of his privacy. As Andy Soltis observed, 'Few people were permitted to know the real Reshevsky.' Although he wrote an autobiography, *Reshevsky on Chess*, published in 1948 (allegedly ghostwritten by Fred Reinfeld), the coverage of his early life in Poland is only briefly touched upon, select snapshots really, and even then pretty much holding to the stock version of events, many details of which changed considerably over time, often from week to week. There remain many unanswered questions, mostly about his family and early life in Poland but specifically his *real* age.

How old was Sammy... really?

'To achieve world-wide fame at the age of eight is a mixed blessing.' Those are Sammy's opening words in his autobiography. But what if he *wasn't* eight? Would that change our views about him?

Speculations about Sammy's age are nothing new. As early as 1920, when Sammy first arrived in New York, there were suspicions. Not because of his size (many thought he could be even younger!) but because of his facial features and demeanour, which caused some to think he might be quite a bit older than advertised. For example, at Sammy's exhibition in Philadelphia in January 1921, Walter Penn Shipley described him as 'slightly built, having the physical appearance of a child of about seven, but his face appeared the face of a child of 10 or 11 years of age.' Dr. Henry Keller, an orthopaedic surgeon at the same event, thought Sammy was 'three years ahead of his age in mentality.' And there were many accounts of people thinking there was something odd about his face, especially his eyes, which 'caused some to shudder', thinking him more like 'midgets who are like children in nothing but stature.' 'Creepy' was how Brian Harley put it. One reporter even suggested his face contains 'all of

Samuel Reshevsky

Born: May 26?, 1909
Died: April 4, 1992

Career highlights

1917	'Discovered' at Warsaw chess club by Akiba Rubinstein
1920	Start of European and US exhibition tours with his parents
1935	Margate, 1st, beats Capablanca
1936	Nottingham, =3rd
1936	First of 8 US Championship titles
1937	Kemeri, =1st
1937	Stockholm Olympiad, Gold with USA
1937/38	Hastings, 1st
1938	AVRO, the Netherlands =4th
1942	Beats Kashdan in match 7½-3½
1948	The Hague/Moscow =3rd
1952	Beats Najdorf in match 11-7
1952	Beats Gligoric in match 5½-4½
1953	Zurich Candidates =2nd
1955	Moscow USSR-USA beats Botvinnik 2½-1½
1960	Beats Benko in match 5½-4½
1960	Buenos Aires 1st
1961	Match against Fischer unfinished at 5½-5½
1969	Netanya 1st
1969	US Championship 8th and last win
1971	US Championship =1st loses playoff to R. Byrne
1974	Nice Olympiad Bronze with USA
1984	Reykjavik Open 1st

the judgment and some of the weariness of forty-five.' There were also reports of Sammy getting annoyed at being referred to as 'a child'.

But in the 1990s other information started percolating to the surface, no doubt in the wake of Sammy's death on April 4, 1992. In the August 1992 *Chess Life* Andy Soltis revealed that Reshevsky had told a number of chess players that he was actually born in 1909 and *not* in 1911. Unfortunately, Soltis did not identify these individuals. However, it is plausible. Reshevsky was known on occasion to inadvertently spill the beans about other 'secrets' from his past, such as the assertion that he had never studied chess as a child, which is simply not true, only to later try to shove the genie back in the bottle.

The 1999 edition of the American National Biography encyclopaedia made a definitive leap, giving Reshevsky's birthday as November 26, 1909, stating in no uncertain terms that 'His year of birth is often incorrectly given as 1911, an inaccuracy brought about by Reshevsky's parents' desire to make their child seem even more extraordinary than he was.' Given the implications of such a pejorative statement, it makes you think the research team must have found *something* tangible to support it. However, no such proof is given.

According to the 'official' record Samuel (Shmuel) Rzeszewski was born on *November 26, 1911* in Ozorków, a small *shtetl* near Lodz in central Poland, which at that time was still part of Imperial Russia during the reign of Tsar Nicholas II. His father was Jakob Rzeszewski, mother Szajndel, married in Lodz 1897. Sammy was the fifth of six children. It is commonly thought Sammy was the youngest, which is not true. He had a little sister, Tauba, born on May 4, 1912.

Already we have a problem. Sammy's stated birthday does not play nice with Tauba's! If both are true that would mean Tauba would have to have been born *at least* four months premature, which would be a landmark case for medical literature. Somebody's birthday cannot be right here.

During Sammy's Tour there was a pervasive agenda by Sammy's father and later his manager, Charles Azenberg, to portray Sammy as younger than he was. To accomplish this they moved his birth year up to

Lodz registration cards from 1919 and 1920 showing Sammy's birth year as 1909 along with each of his siblings' birth years. A later second card corroborates the dates on the first.

1911 and in at least two cases 1912! Interestingly, media accounts rarely give November as his birth month. I found only a single citation and another for December, neither with a specific day. Instead it was almost always May! I found three specific dates: May 16, May 25 and May 26, all in 1911. The third date almost certainly was given by his father.

The question about Sammy's birthday being given as May 26th then becomes: why? Changing the birth year to 1911 to make Sammy appear younger is one thing, but if his birthday was in November then why would they tell people it is in May, which would increase his age by six months? Unless, of course, if May was the real month Sammy was born! This would immediately resolve the timing problem with Tauba, since Sammy could easily have been born on May 26, 1911 and Tauba on May 4,

1912 without conflict. But then if that is true why change it to November 26 later on, in America?

I have a theory. There was no race to be the youngest grandmaster back in 1920 like we have today. What they *did* have was a living legend in José Capablanca! Like Reshevsky, Capablanca had learned to play chess while 'watching his father' play, but instead of at age 5 – as Sammy was originally touted – Capa had done it at age 4! Changing Sammy's birth year from 1909 to 1911 would have made him four as well. However, Capablanca would *still* have the bragging rights as the 'youngest child prodigy in history' since his birthday was on November 19th! Therefore, by changing Sammy's birthday to November 26 he would 'beat' Capa's age by seven days.

Lodz registration cards

The final piece in the puzzle is not circumstantial, but hard evidence of Sammy's true birth year. It is something many people have been in search of for a long time. While it still falls short of official birth records (which may be lost to history), it nevertheless provides compelling evidence, especially since I also discovered a second document corroborating the first, and recently even a third record has surfaced, thanks to Jeff Wexler's research on holocaust records from World War II. I should also mention that Marek Soszynski discovered some of the same information independently and has included at least one of the documents in the digital release of his new book, *The Great Reshevsky: Chess Prodigy & Old Warrior* (2018).

During World War I, much of Poland came under German control, including the city of Lodz where Sammy and most of his family moved after the war began in 1914. During the occupation the Germans began recording all residents of the city, regardless of whether it was their legal residence or not. Their information was recorded on registration cards, some of which have survived and are available at JRI-Poland.org (Jewish Records Indexing for Poland).

The first card is from Sammy's mother, Szajndel, from 1919. And there it is! This clearly and unequivocally shows Szmul (Samuel) was born in 1909!

Acting as Devil's Advocate, Jeff Wexler – who is related to Reshevsky, by marriage, going back to the 1910s – suggested that it could have been a scribal error. Maybe the clerk got it wrong? Perhaps. And yet a year or so later a second registration card was filled out, this time showing the eldest son, Binem, listed as head of household. Szajndel and Szmul are not on it, no doubt because they had already left the country on Sammy's grand chess tour. But it is revealing nonetheless, and corroborates the first, as all of the other dates line up precisely with the first card.

A third corroboration, in part, comes from vital records of Jews in the Lodz Ghetto during World War II. All but one of Sammy's siblings died in the holocaust. However, only a specific date has been found for one, Marjanna, who died March 9, 1941. Her birth year on the Ghetto record was listed as 1903, which again matches the earlier registration cards from two decades earlier.

Conclusion: Reshevsky's birthday should – at the bare minimum – be adjusted to November 26, 1909. And in all probability his actual date of birth was May 26, 1909, adding an additional six months to his age.

The next question, of course, is what do those two years (or 2½ years) mean for Reshevsky's legacy? It means we can give Reshevsky credit for the incredible amount of hard work he invested to become the legendary player he was. As Andy Soltis said, 'It makes his later accomplishments – such as finishing first in a US Championship at age 61 – even more remarkable, since he was actually two years older.'

The dark side: Jekyll and Hyde

But if it wasn't some innate 'gift' from the heavens, then what was it that made him so great? With the exception of Bobby Fischer and possibly Alexander Alekhine, no other player has been both revered and reviled in the same breath as much as Samuel Reshevsky. From his very first international tournament (his very first game!) as an insecure 23 year-old former prodigy at Pasadena 1932 until well into his 70s at Lugano 1987, he was a controversial figure. Most instances had to do with his religion and his unwillingness to play chess on the Sabbath (the Jewish day of rest), but there were many other incidents that tested the limits of ethical behaviour. Some of these were head-scratchers, petty, like humming, fiddling with candy wrappers or blowing smoke while the opponent was on move. Others were much worse, such as illegally starting his opponent's clock even though it was *his* move. And still others were so egregious they make you wonder how Sammy didn't wake up in an alley one day, bloodied and beaten to a pulp, such as at the 1942 US Championship, where Sammy lost on time against Arnold Denker, but the tournament director forfeited *Denker* instead after picking up the clock and turning it toward himself (thereby reversing the clock faces relative to the players). Incredibly, despite 'a

From his very first tournament game until well into his 70s, Sammy Reshevsky was involved in incidents that tested the limits of ethical behaviour.

strong teenage players he deemed a threat.

Above all else Sammy hated to lose. Of course no one likes to lose, but for Sammy it was visceral, like he was being castrated. Even in completely hopeless positions he would drag games out to adjournment just to avoid admitting defeat. If the game was still on-going he had not lost. And maybe the opponent might die

'They make you wonder how Sammy didn't wake up in an alley one day, bloodied and beaten to a pulp.'

near riot' of protests, the decision stood... and Sammy was *good* with that and actually went on to win the tournament as a result!

In my opinion there are two things that transformed Reshevsky into Mr. Hyde. Even *more* contentious than religion: 1) Losing, and 2) Playing against other 'child prodigies' or very

or oversleep, as Reuben Fine did at Pasadena 1932, the first of many future conflicts with Fine.

This aversion to losing can be traced back to his prodigy days, where a loss – even one – was seen as a huge stain on his performance. Many of his exhibitions started in the late evening and thus required adjudications after a few hours play (probably by design). The problem was that Sammy was allowed to solicit, argue and frequently dictate the adjudications. If he was clearly worse he would 'concede' a draw. If he thought he was better (even slightly better with equal material) he would demand the win and if he didn't get it he would pout or cry.

He would also make draw offers in clearly lost positions, fully expecting his adult opponents to acquiesce (which they often did).

One example will suffice, from his exhibition at the *Sinai Social Club* in Milwaukee, set up by Edward Lasker on March 14, 1921.

Reshevsky-Hardiman, 1921

In the above position Black has just played 32...a5. The diagram is correct. White is a full knight down without a hint of compensation. Charles Hardiman later wrote: '...he looked at me saying "I give draw". We shook hands, I could not let go until I kissed his hand, if given good care, he will give to the chess world much as did Paul Morphy, and will trim them all.'

Such incidents were not unusual. The 'he's just a little boy' complex was always in play, as was the 'spirit of chivalry' which prompted many adjudications in his favour simply because he was a boy. Which is probably why Sammy didn't like playing against other children. One, because *he* was the child star; and two, because that adult vs child psychological advantage evaporated when it was another 'little boy' sitting across from him.

Pictureland

This was never more on display than when Sammy visited Los Angeles in the Summer of 1921. Of all the destinations on his tour, 'Pictureland' surely takes the prize for being both the most famous and most infamous. Famous because this is where Sammy met the legendary actor Charlie Chaplin. Infamous because Sammy faced not just one but two 'Boy Wonders' and lost to both!

One man among the large crowd of onlookers who met Sammy at the train station was Harry Borochow (1898-1993), the 'Flower of Los Angeles Chess' who would go on to win the California state championship many times over and become one of the state's most prominent promotors of chess. He set up Sammy's exhibitions, chaperoned him around Los Angeles, and famously brought the boy by the movie studio to meet Charlie Chaplin for whom Borochow was working as a film splicer. It was Borochow, in fact, who snapped the now famous photos of Reshevsky with Chaplin and Douglas Fairbanks on the set of *The Three Musketeers* (1921). In his autobiography Chaplin famously described his encounter with the boy with the 'intense little face with large eyes that stare belligerently'.

Sammy's first exhibition was held at the Los Angeles Athletic Club on June 27th against 20 opponents. His final tally was an impressive 14 wins and 6 draws. But that doesn't begin to tell the whole story! One of Sammy's opponents was a 16 year-old boy named Donald Mugridge, who was something of a local chess celebrity, even nicknamed the 'Boy Wonder of Los Angeles chess'. During the exhibition Sammy finished off most opponents fairly effortlessly, but was having a tougher time against a few others, including Borochow, Dr. Robert Griffith and Mugridge.

Hollywood 1921. Child film star Jackie Coogan and Sammy Reshevsky face off in a boxing pose. A moment later Jackie punches Sammy in the eye!

'Chaplin famously described his encounter with the boy with the "intense little face with large eyes that stare belligerently".'

According to Borochow, at 11 pm Sammy's manager announced that 'play would continue until 12'. But 'at about 11:15 Sammy came to my board, where I had an apparent win, whispered to his manager, who then announced adjudication would begin now.' While Borochow and Dr. Griffith were allowed to adjudicate each other's games, all others were adjudicated by Sammy's manager, Charles Azenberg! Dr. Griffith was up a knight for two pawns with the better position so Borochow awarded him the win. Sammy rejected this, saying 'We will play that game out!' Borochow also claimed a win, which Dr. Griffith awarded. Rejecting that also, Sammy 'studied my game for about 15 minutes', said Borochow, and 'demonstrated a forced draw'.

Meanwhile, Mugridge was up a pawn with the better position and claimed a win, which Azenberg would not concede, and he declared the game drawn. A now angry Mugridge then demanded the game be played out, like Dr. Griffith's, but this too was declined. Draw! The following day Mugridge was one of the first to arrive at Hamburger's department store where Sammy's second exhibition was scheduled, against 12 opponents. This time Mugridge did beat Sammy! According to Borochow, when Sammy lost he 'burst out crying, sobbing to me, "I wouldn't mind if I lost to an older man, but to a little boy..."' 1-0 Mugridge!

It would be nearly a week before the adjourned game against Dr. Griffith was finally played out. Charlie Chaplin came to watch the game and brought 5 year-old child actor Jackie Coogan to meet Sammy. Coogan was Chaplin's co-star in the movie,

The Kid, then being filmed, though others may remember him best as Uncle Fester in the 1960s comedy, *The Addams Family*. Before the chess started, Jackie and Sammy posed for several photos, including one where they are pretending to be boxing. But Jackie had other ideas and he punched Sammy in the eye and Sammy burst out crying. Sammy wanted to fight for real but Jackie was whisked away. Revenge denied! 1-0 Coogan!

Both of these encounters had a powerful effect on Sammy. Even years later he spoke disparagingly of Mugridge, who had since graduated from Harvard and was working as an archivist at the National Archives in Washington D.C. And Coogan? For months afterward Sammy talked about him, how 'fresh' he was, and how he wanted revenge. He never got it!

And the game against Dr. Griffith? When the position was adjourned it had been *before* Sammy had come to Dr. Griffith's board, so it should have been the doctor's move. But Sammy insisted it was *his* move! Good-natured that he was, Dr. Griffith finally gave in, allowing Sammy to move a second time in succession. Dr. Griffith did not respond well and a few moves later blundered and actually lost the game!

What made Reshevsky... Reshevsky?

Objectively, there was nothing brilliant or even particularly creative about Reshevsky's play. He was not a surgeon wielding a scalpel like Alekhine; rather more like a lumberjack swinging his axe, chips flying, until the tree finally topples. There are no 'Evergreens' or 'Gold Coin'

immortals in his canon. There are not even any openings or variations that bear his name. As Anthony Santasiere put it, 'he was a genius using his talent not so much to create, but to conquer. It was not the beauty or the idea that mattered, but the point.' In fact, if you compare him to the likes of Capablanca, Botvinnik, or his compatriots Fischer and Reuben Fine, Sammy's play wasn't even particularly accurate or refined. He was not a strategist, though he is often placed in that category. What he did have – in spades – was an incredible command of tactics and unmatched grit. Arnold Denker famously described playing against Sammy as 'like trying to shake off a pitbull that clamped its teeth on the leg of your trousers.'

He also had a herculean capacity for suffering. You simply could not demoralize Reshevsky. No matter how bad his position looked he would fight and fight and fight.

It may seem odd to say it, but all the negative aspects of growing up as a child prodigy undoubtedly contributed to his later manifestation as a world champion calibre player. In fact I believe that is what most defined him! It was his dark side and the panoply of edgy traits that made him nearly as hated as he was admired. No one feared Reshevsky for the technical strength of his play. But what Reshevsky brought to the table was an indomitable spirit, a Rocky Marciano that just keeps bulling ahead no matter how many times you hit him. That 'fight' could be controlled to some extent in tournament conditions – and like with Fischer, entire 'tournament strategies' were designed to do just that – but in a match setting that element disappears and you are left facing the foul-tempered rodent head-on. For his entire life Reshevsky lived as if backed into a corner, fighting for survival itself, making him the most dangerous animal of all. ∎

Judit Polgar

The Pawn Umbrella

Advanced enemy pawns can be menacing and dangerous. But, as **JUDIT POLGAR** shows, they may also serve as an umbrella, offering your king unexpected safety and protection.

That the pawns are the soul of chess has been known since the middle of the 18th century. In 1749, André Danican Philidor came to this conclusion in his seminal work *L'Analyze des Échecs*, which saw an English translation, *Chess Analysed*, a year later. But, depending on factors such as style, level of understanding and experience, players relate to pawns in different ways.

When I was a kid, I thought that pawns mainly served to be advanced en masse to support your attacking pieces, or to be sacrificed for clearing files and diagonals, or simply for the initiative.

The first phase of the next game fragment is a good illustration of my approach at the time. But after a few more moves we will reach a position that is typical for the main theme that we will examine in this column.

'This is a paradoxical situation: one of the players can use an enemy pawn as a shield for his or her king.'

Xie Jun
Judit Polgar
Thessaloniki Olympiad 1988

position after 20.♔g1

Barely out of the opening, I had sacrificed a pawn to open the h-file for my rooks and to weaken the long diagonal by exchanging White's light-squared bishop. My next move was meant to clear even more space for my pieces, viz. the fourth rank and the h1-a8 and h2-b8 diagonals. Could one ask for more?

20...g5! 21.fxg5 ♗xe4 22.♕f2?
This seemingly active move is the decisive mistake. Since my pawn break also cleared the f-file, Xie Jun decided to use it to gain time for a regrouping with ♘e3 and ♖ae1. White should have continued her development without delay with

22.♘f2, e.g. 22...♗b7 23.♖ad1 ♕c6 24.♕g3, and White has parried the immediate threats.

22...f5!!
When I met Xie Jun again, a few decades later, she confessed that she still remembered the shock caused by this move.

23.gxf6+ ♔f7
The situation has radically changed, and Black is winning. The advanced and seemingly dangerous white f-pawn is in fact acting as an 'umbrella' for the black king, completely neutralizing White's play along the f-file. Having neglected her development two moves earlier, White will not have time to regroup in order to parry the combined threats of my pieces.

This paradoxical situation, when one

of the players can use an enemy pawn as a shield for his or her king, will be the main theme of this article.

24.♕e3
If I had defended the f7-pawn with 22...♖8h7, White would have done well after 24.♘e3, but with the queen's rook freed from defensive tasks, Black wins with 24...♖xh3! 25.gxh3 ♖xh3.

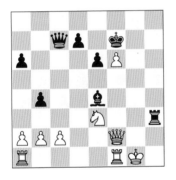

With her last move, White has somehow consolidated h3, but in doing so she has weakened the second rank, allowing a different combination.
24...♗xg2! 25.♕g5
A desperate attempt at counterplay. If 25.♔xg2 then 25...♖g8+ 26.♔f2 ♕xc2+ wins, e.g. 27.♔e1 ♖e4 or 27.♕e2 ♖g2+!.
25...♖4h7
25...♖g8 was more precise.
26.♔xg2 ♖g8
And I won on move 53.

Fifteen years later I faced a similar situation in a rapid game, but this time I was on the receiving end.

Vishy Anand
Judit Polgar
Mainz (rapid) 2003

position after 35...♕c7

White has several reasons to boast an advantage. He has an extra pawn and a promising kingside attack, and several black pawns will be vulnerable in the endgame. But I still cherished hope in view of the pressure on c2, which I intended to increase with ...♖c6, after which, in an extreme case, I might even dream of ...♕c3-a1 mate. But Anand's next move puts an end to my attacking ideas.
36.c4! bxc3 37.♔c2
The king is now safely defended by my c-pawn and White can proceed with his attack. Moreover, after simplifications the pawns on a3 and c3 would be doomed.
37...♖d6 38.♖d1 g6 39.♕g4 ♖cd8 40.♖dd3 ♗b6
I did my best to get some counterplay, but since the white bishop is defending d2, creating threats is not simple.
41.♕h4 h5 42.gxh6 ♔h7

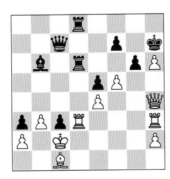

With my last few moves I have opened an umbrella for my own king, too.

This is actually a typical reaction against White's attack along the h-file in the Sicilian. But my king is far less safe than White's, since g7 is not defended by my bishop, and the seventh rank will soon be weaker than the second one. Besides, the a3- and c3-pawns are weak, whereas the one on h6 is not.
43.♖xd6 ♕xd6 44.fxg6+ fxg6 45.♕g4 ♕d4 46.♕e2
There was little I could do against threats like ♖f3 or ♖d3, and Anand won (1-0, 60).

In the examples above, neither Xie Jun nor I would have been able to avoid the king's pawn umbrella scenario, but sometimes, it is allowed by one of the players miscalculating.

Ljubomir Ljubojevic
Arturo Pomar
Las Palmas 1975

position after 22.♘d3

The annoying pawn on f3 gives Black good reason to boast compensation for the minor material disadvantage of being a pawn down.
22...fxg2?
A serious mistake. The pawn's proximity to the white king looks threatening, but it actually prevents Black from creating threats against White's Achilles' heel, g2. One important detail is that Black will not have time to bring his knight close to the h3- or f3-square.
Simplest would have been 22...♕g4! 23.♘e1 (defending g2 and e4) 23...fxg2 24.♗e3 (unlike in the game, 24.♗c3 does not work due to

24...♗xc3, when 25.♕xc3? ♖xf2! wins, while 25.bxc3 ♘c4 offers Black a strong initiative) 24...♘d7. After the knight's retreat from d3 Black can use the e5-square for his own knight: 25.f3 ♕h3, with excellent black counterplay.
23.♕b3+ ♔h8

White played **24.♗c3** and eventually won, but even stronger would have been 24.♖xc6 ♖ad8 25.♗c3 ♕f3 26.♖c7, with a decisive attack. Black's helplessness to create effective threats against the white king is desolating.

Diversifying a bit, in the next game, the *pas-de-deux* of the black king and the umbrella pawn takes place close to the chess board's equator.

Heinrich Wolf
Akiba Rubinstein
Teplitz-Schönau 1922

position after 37...♕d8

Black's structure is better. The knight stands superbly on c5, and the a-pawn is likely to become dangerous. In order to reach a strategically winning position, he still needs to block the g4-pawn.

38.♖b1?
White should have other priorities than defending the b-file. He should have taken measures against the blockade with 38.g5!, activating the bishop at the same time: 38...♗b8 (if 38...♖b8, White has 39.c4, preparing to meet 39...♖b2 with 40.c3) 39.♗f5 ♕b6 40.♔g2, followed by ♔h3, and White has every chance to maintain approximate equality.
38...♖b8! 39.♖b4 a6

40.♔e2
40.g5 is no longer effective, now that the white rook has left the first rank, since it would make the pawn vulnerable: 40...♖b6!?. Defending c7 and threatening ...♕xg5, with a decisive attack, e.g. 41.♗g4 h3 42.♗xh3 ♕xg5 43.♗g2 ♕g3+ 44.♔f1 ♘xe4 45.fxe4 f3 46.♗xf3 ♕xf3+ 47.♔g1 ♕d1+ (it is useful to collect the c2-pawn with check) 48.♔g2 ♕xc2+ 49.♔g1 ♕xc3 50.♕a4 ♖b5!? 51.♖xb5 axb5. In the absence of the c2-pawn, 52.♕xb5 ♕c5+ 53.♕xc5 dxc5 wins easily.
40...♖b6 41.♕a1

41...♔g6!!

Having stabilized the queenside, Black improves his kingside position.
42.♔d2 ♔g5

The king is best suited to block the g-pawn, leaving the queen free for queenside operations. The g-pawn offers His Majesty absolute safety and turns the white bishop into a mere spectator. Activating it with ♗f1-c4 would free the h4-pawn's path.
43.♖b1 ♕b8 44.♖h1 a5!

45.♗g2
45.♕xa5 loses to 45...♖b2, threatening ...♘b3+, because now that the queen has departed from a1, ♔c1 allows ...♖b1+. And if 46.♕a3 then 46...♘b3+ 47.♔d1 ♖b1+.
45...a4
And Black won.

Conclusion
■ When facing a massive attack, the possibility of using an enemy pawn as a shield or umbrella for your king can be very effective.
■ However, when you are attacking, you should reckon with the possibility that your opponent will use the same method! ■

NEW FRITZ-TRAINER DVDs

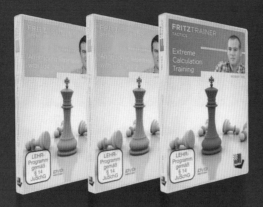

Let GM Nicholas Pert provide you with a fighting 1.d4 repertoire with his two new DVDs. Master Robert Ris' interactive DVD "Extreme Calculation" and become a great calculator at the board!

NICHOLAS PERT:
AN ATTACKING REPERTOIRE WITH 1.d4 – PART ONE (1.d4 d5 2.c4)

In this detailed "two-part" video series Pert takes a look at a main line White system based on 1.d4. This series is aimed at the ambitious player who is looking to put maximum pressure on their opponent from the start of the game. In this DVD he considers positions in which Black plays with an early d5. The start position for this DVD is 1.d4 d5 2.c4. This series has many chapters and is a thorough analysis, showing how to fight for the advantage from positions in which Black plays with an early d5. This is a high-level opening choice with many fresh ideas designed to cause problems for Black players in their pet opening systems. 1.d4 d5 2.c4 has been played by practically all of the World's leading players at some point in their chess careers. The bulk of this 39 chapter DVD considers how to tackle the Queen's Gambit Accepted, Queen's Gambit Declined and Slav Defence. In addition I examine the Triangle system, 2...c5, Tarrasch Defense, Henning-Shara Gambit, Baltic Defense, Chigorin and Albin Counter-Gambit.

29,90 €

NICHOLAS PERT:
AN ATTACKING REPERTOIRE WITH 1.d4 – PART TWO (1.d4 Nf6 2.c4)

The second volume focuses on a White system against openings such as the "Nimzo-Indian", Benoni and Benko. Please note that the Grunfeld and Kings Indian variations (2...g6) are not covered in this DVD. There are many aggressive, fresh ideas designed to cause problems for Black players. "My chosen lines tend to be very attacking, aiming to quickly fight for control of the centre and an early attack on the black king. There is also a lot of original analysis included. This video series considers how to tackle the "Nimzo-Indian" using the move 4.Qc2. Various Benoni lines are considered, the main line, Czech, Snake, Late and Old Benoni. Some fresh, aggressive, attacking ideas have been considered against the Benko Gambit and Blumenfeld. In addition I have looked at how to play against 2...b6, the Budapest and Fajarowicz."

29,90 €

ROBERT RIS:
EXTREME CALCULATION TRAINING

After the success of the first volume on Calculation Training, Dutch IM Robert Ris continues with "Extreme Calculation Training" — a wide range of new aspects which have to be mastered to become a great calculator at the board! The topics discussed in the original series (candidate moves, method of elimination & imagination) are certainly useful when studying the content of this new video series. Special attention will be paid to intermediate moves, quiet moves, sacrifices on empty squares, mating patterns, ignoring opponent threats, calculation in defence and methods of comparison. On top of that, more practical advice for training is recommended, for instance how to handle your time management and how to visualise the position in your mind during the calculation process. After going through the 13 examples from the theoretical section, it's time to switch the brain to active participation and your calculation skills will be tested seriously! The frequent request for more puzzles has been granted, as Ris has selected no less than 50 games with multiple questions. After all, training your calculation abilities is an activity which never ends; it takes continual practise to stay sharp at the board!

29,90 €

ChessBase GmbH · News: en.chessbase.com · CB Shop: shop.chessbase.com
CHESSBASE DEALER: NEW IN CHESS · P.O. Box 1093 · NL-1810 KB Alkmaar NEW IN CHESS ChessBase
phone (+31)72 5127137 · fax (+31)72 5158234 · WWW.NEWINCHESS.COM

Hikaru Nakamura claims Grand Chess Tour in blitz game

Classical chess takes back seat at London Classic

Hikaru Nakamura knows he is the winner of the London Classic and the Grand Chess Tour. MVL's queen is trapped and he cannot take the bishop because of the knight fork on h6.

The London Classic, the last leg of the 2018 Grand Chess Tour, introduced a new format with fewer participants and a mix of classical, rapid and blitz. Possibly inspired by the 'London System' that Magnus Carlsen used to defend his title, the players avoided great risks in the classical games, drawing them all. A win against Maxime Vachier-Lagrave in the fourth blitz game of the final brought Hikaru Nakamura first place and overall victory in the GCT. The British KO Championship, held at the same time, saw one decisive classical game, won by the ultimate winner Gawain Jones. **JON SPEELMAN** reports from the British capital.

NOTES BY
Hikaru Nakamura

It was in 2009 that Malcolm Pein first held a top class tournament at Kensington Olympia in West London. With the help of an anonymous sponsor, who continued his support right up to last year, four of the world's absolute elite came to London to do battle together with four of Britain's very best with the inaugural honours going to Magnus Carlsen, who was first ahead of Vladimir Kramnik.

Nine years later, the London Classic has become established as the final event of the Grand Chess Tour. This year it welcomed a new sponsor, the Lohia Foundation, a charitable trust founded by Indian businessman ML Lohia; and also a new format which whittled the Classic down to just the top four in the GCT.

These four contested a knockout finale and the tradition of elite players foreign and British persisted as they played in parallel with the semi-finals and finals of the British Knockout Championship. Both events comprised two classical, two rapidplay and four blitz games. A win in the classical games was worth 6 points, for rapid and blitz this was 4 and 2 points.

The tournaments were held in two halves with the semi-finals at Google DeepMind and the finals at Olympia itself. DeepMind is the company founded by Demis Hassabis and two others – and acquired by Google in 2014 – which created AlphaGo and more recently AlphaZero. The building, which is close to King's Cross station, now serves as Google's UK headquarters and is an impressive edifice with, as you might expect from a world leader in AI, scrupulous security: which meant that attendance was by invitation only.

The playing venue, which was also used a couple of times last year, was a nice theatre/lecture hall and outside there were copious snacks and an analysis room where Dan King and Lawrence Trent presided. Next to the hospitality area there was a small improvised studio where Alejandro Ramirez did interviews for the show being broadcast from the GCT's headquarters in St. Louis.

For the finals, they moved across town to the Classic's original venue, Kensington Olympia, a huge complex which holds events such as the 'Horse of the Year Show'. The Classic uses the whole of a single floor which includes the theatre where the games are played, a large side hall which accommodates the annual International Open and a large area with a bookstall where people can mill around and with plenty of room for simultaneous displays in the middle.

'It made the classical games so crucial that not losing became more critical than winning.'

There is also a hall which serves as the commentary room and next to it a VIP room with commentary by Julian Hodgson, which is where I normally hide and heckle with co-conspirators often including John Nunn.

All draws

The results of both events you can see in the tables. The melding of classical, rapidplay and blitz on a weighted basis is an interesting idea, but in practice it made the classical games so crucial that, perhaps, not losing became more critical than winning. All eight of the classical games of the GCT were drawn with the decisive action deferred to the rapidplay. And in the final between Hikaru Nakamura and Maxime Vachier-Lagrave the decision came in the very final game of the blitz. Here's that key game with comments by the winner.

Hikaru Nakamura
Maxime Vachier-Lagrave
London 2018 (blitz-4)
English Opening, Symmetrical Variation

This critical 4th blitz game was important, as I had White and the chance to end the match without any further tiebreaks or Armageddon madness. Prior to this game, I had played the same variation twice within this English/Grünfeld without success, having narrowly missed a win in the 1st rapid game and then getting into a little trouble in the 2nd blitz game. As such, it was imperative that I try to come up with something to surprise Maxime. Having only about ten minutes before the game and only smartphones, we (he and his second Kris Littlejohn – ed.) were able to come up with a very small idea with a lot of bite. It truly is a wonderful time to be alive!

1.♘f3 c5 2.c4 ♘f6 3.♘c3 d5 4.cxd5 ♘xd5 5.e3 ♘xc3 6.bxc3 g6 7.♗b5+ ♗d7 8.♗e2 ♗g7 9.0-0 0-0 10.d4

10...♗c6!?

10...♕a5 was seen in Gelfand-Nepomniachtchi in Zurich 2017. The game ended in a draw, but there were chances for both sides: 11.♕b3 ♗c6 12.♗d2 ♘d7 13.c4?! (after 13.d5 ♗a4 14.♕a3 b5 15.♖ab1 ♕a6 there is a completely balanced position, but I felt that perhaps Black's pieces are a bit more awkward and the ideas are not as straightforward especially in a quicker game) 13...♕a6 14.♗c3 ♖ab8, and Black was already completely fine, which is why my idea was to play the aforementioned 13.d5.

10...♘c6 was what Maxime tried in his previous match against Levon Aronian, and despite being able to houdini his way into a draw, he was completely lost in that game: 11.♖b1 ♕c7 12.e4 ♗g4 13.d5 ♘e5 14.c4 b6 15.♘xe5 ♗xe2 16.♕xe2 ♗xe5 17.f4 ♗d4+ 18.♔h1 e6 19.e5 exd5 20.cxd5 ♕d7 21.d6, and White has an overwhelming position.

11.♗a3 cxd4 12.cxd4 ♖e8

13.♖c1 The original idea which won me the London Chess Classic.

In the two previous games, I tried 13.♘e5 and while I got something in the first game, by the time of the second game, Maxime had found the improvements.

13.♘e5 ♕a5, and now:

ANALYSIS DIAGRAM

A) 14.♘xc6 ♕xa3 15.♘xb8 (15.♘e5 ♗xe5 16.dxe5 e6 is what we reached in the second blitz game, and despite being able to draw, I was in a touch of trouble) 15...♖axb8, and White has a symbolic advantage, but Black is completely fine.

B) 14.♕b3 ♗xe5 15.dxe5 ♕xe5 16.♗c4

ANALYSIS DIAGRAM

B1) 16...♖f8?! 17.f4 ♕e4 18.♖f2 ♘d7 19.♖d1 b5 20.♗e2 ♕a4 21.♕xa4

bxa4 22.♗a6. In this position White stands much better, as I proved in the second rapid game, but when I missed this opportunity, the whole situation changed, which is much like how modern chess is. You get one shot to make an idea work before a change is required.

B2) 16...e6!. A strange move, as it looks like opening the long diagonal from a1 to h8 will lead to a mate, but computers, as they often do, prove that just about everything is fine even if it looks suicidal: 17.♗b2 ♕a5 18.e4 ♘d7 19.♕e3 ♕b6 20.♕c3 e5 21.♖ab1 ♘f6. Even though this looks super scary for Black, with threats on both of the long diagonals, the computer shows that the position is still balanced.

13...♕a5

A logical move which tries to follow the plans from before, but in this position it is simply a bad move.

14.♕b3 ♘d7 15.♗b4!

15...♕f5 After 15...♕a4 16.♕b1 ♖ac8 17.h3, White is still better, but this would have been a better try than in the game.

15...♕b6 16.a3 is also slightly unpleasant.

16.♗d3! ♕h5 17.e4!

All of these moves have been straight-forward with simple ideas, which is extremely important in blitz games as it is important to get as deep into the game as you can (with either colour) without having to think a lot.

17...e6 18.h3

A restrictive move, which also creates luft for the king if needed.

18...♖ad8 19.♖fe1 a5 20.♗d2 a4 21.♕b1 ♖c8

22.♗e2!

Another nice touch. 22.♔h2 also wins, but as I had looked into this previous variation before the game with a computer, I knew that ♗e2 was just as strong.

22...♗f6 23.♖cd1

Not necessary, but Black doesn't have any useful moves.

23...♖ed8 24.♘g5 ♕h4 25.g3 ♕h6 26.♘xf7 ♕xh3

27.♗f1?!

As soon as I went ♗f1, I realized right away that ♗g4 was possible, and I was fortunate enough to be able to repeat moves, with Maxime being unable to avoid the picturesque finish.

27...♕h5 28.♗e2 ♕h3 29.♗g4

Here Maxime resigned in view of the fork on h6. Thus, I won the game and finished as the 2018 Grand Chess Tour Champion!

■ ■ ■

The knockout format creates raw excitement which is more visceral than a mere tournament table, but the very tension that it creates can sometimes rather backfire. Following Magnus Carlsen's example in the

'It truly is a wonderful time to be alive!' Having only ten minutes before the 4th blitz game against MVL and only smartphones, Hikaru Nakamura and his second Kris Littlejohn came up with a 'very small idea with a lot of bite'.

World Championship match, an impression has been created that the best way for his peers to cope with Fabiano Caruana is to draw classical games and then hope to prevail at faster time limits. Both Nakamura and Aronian played very tamely against Caruana's Petroff in their second classical game. Though admittedly fighting against his preparation at the moment is a huge task.

Knockout matches are fun but, if practicable, I personally would prefer a return to the wonderful all-play-alls that have graced the Classic over the decade. Classical chess is generally of a higher standard than at faster time limits and more players means more games per round – the more the merrier. That being said, there was, of course, plenty of action at Google DeepMind and Olympia.

The novelty that Fabiano Caruana comes up with in the following fascinating game was obviously part of his preparation for the World Championship match against Magnus Carlsen and no doubt was backed up by pages of analysis. I'm not going remotely to try to reconstruct this, but will aim to pinpoint the critical positions.

NOTES BY
Jonathan Speelman

**Levon Aronian
Fabiano Caruana**
London Classic 2018 (2.3)
Queen's Gambit Declined,
Blackburne Variation

**1.d4 ♘f6 2.c4 e6 3.♘f3 d5 4.♘c3
♗e7 5.♗f4 0-0 6.e3 c5 7.dxc5
♗xc5 8.♕c2 ♘c6 9.♖d1 ♕a5
10.a3 ♖d8**

The rare move that Caruana used in Game 2 against Carlsen.
11.♘d2 Carlsen played 11.♗e2 ♘e4 12.0-0 ♘xc3 13.bxc3 h6 14.a4 ♘e7 15.♘e5 ♗d6 16.cxd5 ♘xd5 17.♗f3 ♘xf4 18.exf4 ♗xe5 19.♖xd8+ ♕xd8 20.fxe5 ♕c7.

ANALYSIS DIAGRAM

This was already strategically better for Caruana, and Carlsen had to fight for his life before finally escaping (½-½, 49).
11...d4 Obviously the critical move, if it is playable. In previous games Black once played 11...e5, which is a mistake since after ♗g5 and ♗xf6 the knight can often go to d5, and four times the rather wimbly 11...dxc4.

After 11...dxc4 12.♗xc4 ♗e7 there shouldn't be anything very much wrong with Black's position, but presumably White should be able to get += or at least '+==' if he plays really accurately.
While after 11...e5 12.♗g5 dxc4 (12...d4? 13.♗xf6 gxf6 14.♘b3 ♕c7 15.♘d5 ♕d6 16.♗d3 and Black is in trouble) 13.♘xc4 ♕c7 you don't need to go any further than this to know that White is better.
12.♘b3 ♕b6 13.♘a4 ♗b4+!

The point of Caruana's play.
14.axb4 ♕xb4+ 15.♘d2 ♕a5
Black is a piece down for just a single pawn, but will be able to create serious threats with ...♘b4 since White is disorganised and a huge tempo down in development with the bishop still on f1. I actually started following the game here and since Aronian was playing quite quickly didn't get the chance to think too much about alternatives at the time.

16.♕b3
16.b3 is obviously also critical: 16...♘b4 17.♕b2 e5 (17...d3? 18.f3 is simply bad for Black) 18.♗g5 ♗f5

ANALYSIS DIAGRAM

This is extremely dangerous though given as 0.00 by my ever helpful silicon friend. My first reaction was 19.♗xf6? gxf6 20.♗e2 (20.e4 loses to 20...♗xe4 21.♘xe4 ♘d3+ 22.♔e2 ♘xb2 23.♘xb2 f5), but that turns out badly, since the bishop was needed to defend e3: 20...b5 21.cxb5 ♘c2+ 22.♔f1 dxe3 splat! The alternative is 19.♗e2 b5 20.cxb5 ♘c2+ 21.♔f1 dxe3 22.♗xe3 ♖ac8, with a powerful attack.

ANALYSIS DIAGRAM

London 2018 Grand Chess Tour play-off									
Semifinals									
Hikaru Nakamura	3	3	2	4	0	2	2	2	18
Fabiano Caruana	3	3	2	0	2	0	0	0	10
Maxime Vachier-Lagrave	3	3	2	4	2	2	0	2	18
Levon Aronian	3	3	2	0	0	0	2	0	10
Final 3rd/4th place									
Fabiano Caruana	3	3	2	4	0	0	2	2	16
Levon Aronian	3	3	2	0	2	2	0	0	12
Final 1st/2nd place									
Hikaru Nakamura	3	3	2	2	1	1	1	2	15
Maxime Vachier-Lagrave	3	3	2	2	1	1	1	0	13

6 points for a win in Classical, 4 in Rapid, 2 in Blitz

Houdini tells me that 23.♗g5 is best now, with this (logical but extremely complicated) continuation: 23...h6 24.♕xe5 ♖d5 25.♗xf6 ♖xd2 26.♗xg7 ♘d3 27.♖xd2 ♕xd2 28.g3 ♘e3+ 29.♕xe3 ♗xe2+ 30.♔g2 ♕d5+ 31.♔g1 ♕d1+, with a draw.

16...e5 17.♗g5 ♘b4 18.♗e2
18.♗xf6 gxf6 19.♗e2 seems to transpose.

18...♗d7 19.♗xf6

DeepMind co-founder and CEO Demis Hassabis makes the first move for Fabiano Caruana. The American must have gotten the impression that his opponents tried to play as little classical chess against him as possible.

19...gxf6 19...♗xa4? loses material: 20.♖a1 ♗xb3 21.♖xa5 dxe3 22.♗xd8.
20.♖a1 dxe3 21.fxe3 b5
Bashed out by Caruana a tempo.

22.0-0
Aronian played this quickly, and even if he hadn't analysed the line in advance it was an easy decision, since White gets a nice initiative with a safe king. While if he plays 22.cxb5, he'll keep an extra piece for the moment but be in serious danger (from a human perspective): 22...♗e6 23.♕d1 ♖ac8 24.0-0 ♘c2 (from afar you'd also wonder if White has to worry whether 24...♖c2 works, though in fact it doesn't especially well) 25.♘c3! ♘xa1 26.♕e1!. This is playable for White, but certainly not better.

22...bxa4 23.♕c3 f5 24.♘f3 f6 25.♘h4 ♘c6 26.♕a3 e4

Caruana's second Rustam Kasim-dzhanov came into the VIP room round about here and obviously we sought to extract information. While, of course, he could and would not say too much, I think it's likely that we were still following Caruana's analysis if not Aronian's (you might well stop after 23.♕c3 with a pleasant +=).
27.♗d1 27.♕d6 ♕e5 28.♘xf5 ♗xf5 29.♕xc6 is obviously critical. Houdini, which, as anybody who uses it knows, has a habit of evaluating lines as dead equal, gives 29...♕xb2 now as 0.00 after a few seconds: 30.♖ae1 ♕c3 31.♔h1 a3 32.♖a6 ♗c8 33.♕c6 ♗f5.
27...♘e5

28.♗xa4
Rustam said that 28.♕e7 'doesn't win either' (or words to that effect). I guess the line continues something like 28...♕d2 29.♕xf6 ♕xb2 30.♕g5+ ♔h8 31.♕f6+ ♔g8.
28...♕xa4 29.♕xa4 ♗xa4 30.♖xa4

30...f4! This excellent move messes up White's coordination, leading to a defensible position.

31.♖xf4

31.exf4 is the engine's first choice, but looks very ugly to the human eye.

31...♖d1+ 32.♔f1 ♖xf1+ 33.♔xf1 ♖b8 34.b4 ♘xc4 35.♘f5 ♖b5 36.g4 h5 37.h3 hxg4 38.hxg4 ♘e5

Now it all dissolves and the game will be drawn.

39.♖xa7 ♖xb4 40.♔g2 ♖b1 41.♖e7 ♖b2+ 42.♔h3 ♖f2 43.♖e8+ ♔h7 44.♖e7+ ♔g8 45.♖e8+ ♔h7 46.♖e7+ ♔g8
Draw.

∎ ∎ ∎

Gawain Jones was the only player to win a classical game in the British KO, against Luke McShane in the final, and this provided a wonderful platform for him to take the title.

London KO 2018

Quarter Finals	
Adams – Williams	1½-½
Howell – Haria	3-1
Jones – Merry	1½-½
McShane – Hawkins	1½-½

Semi-Finals	
McShane – Adams	16-12
Jones – Howell	18-10

Final 3rd/4th place	
Adams – Howell	16-12

Final 1st/2nd place	
Jones – McShane	21-7

NOTES BY
Gawain Jones

Gawain Jones
Luke McShane
London British Knockout
Championship 2018 (19.1)
French Defence, Tarrasch Variation

1.e4 e6 A slight surprise, but Luke had tried the French in one game in the semi-final with Mickey Adams, so I'd had a brief look.

2.d4 d5 3.♘d2 c5 4.♘gf3 cxd4 5.exd5 ♕xd5 6.♗c4 ♕d7!?
This move looks the most unnatural retreat, but is actually sensible. There are a lot of similarities and transpositions here to the 6....♕d8 lines, but one advantage is that the knight will be defended on c6.

7.0-0 A few days previously Mickey Adams had played 7.♘b3 ♘c6 8.♘bxd4 ♘xd4 9.♘xd4 a6 10.♗f4!? ♘f6 11.0-0 b5 12.♗b3 ♗b7 (12...♗c5 is also played here) 13.♖e1 ♗e7 14.c3 ♘d5 15.♗e5 0-0?! 16.♕g4 and White had a strong initiative and quickly won material, although Luke defended stubbornly and managed a miracle save (Adams-McShane, London 2018).
7...♘c6 8.♘b3 a6

9.a4 Another game between two top English players saw 9.♘bxd4, but Black had absolutely no problems: 9...♘xd4 10.♘xd4 ♕c7 11.♕e2 ♗d6 (I actually had this position once myself, although the queen had come to c7 via d8 there) 12.h3 ♘e7 13.♗e3 0-0 14.♖ad1 b5 15.♗b3 ♘g6 16.c4 bxc4 17.♕xc4 ♗h2+ 18.♔h1 ♕xc4 19.♗xc4 ♗f4 20.♗xf4 ½-½, Adams-Howell, Hull 2018.

9...♘f6 10.♕e2 ♗d6 11.♖d1 e5 12.♘bxd4

12...0-0!
Black's most accurate move order. I'd had this position a few years ago in the Tromsø World Cup. There my opponent went for the more forcing 12...♘xd4 13.♖xd4 ♕e7, but this allows 14.♖xd6!? ♕xd6 15.b3!. With Black's king stuck in the centre, White has very good compensation for the sacrificed exchange: 15...e4 16.♗a3 ♕f4 17.♖e1 (17.♕e1!? is recommended by John Shaw in his *Playing 1.e4* for Quality Chess) 17...♗g4, Jones-Shimanov, Tromsø 2013. This was in the rapid playoff and I couldn't assess the consequences of 18.♗b5+!,

ANALYSIS DIAGRAM

but White would have been doing very well after 18...axb5 19.♕xb5+ ♘d7 (19...♗d7 20.♕c5 and Black can't adequately defend against the mate threat on e7) 20.♕xb7 ♖b8 21.♖xe4+ ♗e6 22.♕xd7+ ♔xd7 23.♖xf4, when White has three connected passed pawns for the exchange and should just be winning. **13.♘xc6 ♕xc6 14.♗g5 ♗c7 15.♗xf6 ♕xf6 16.♗d5**

Quite an interesting position has arisen. Black has the bishop pair and would be comfortably better if the e-pawn were back on e6. However, here White has at least temporary control of the light squares and for now the bishop on c7 is stuck defending the slightly loose e5-pawn. If Black manages to regroup his pieces and get in ...e5-e4, perhaps supported by ...f7-f5, then he will be doing very well, so White has to play accurately.

16...♖b8
Black doesn't actually have to spend the tempo defending his b7-pawn, but can go 16...♗f5 17.♗xb7 (of course, White isn't obliged to take this pawn) 17...♖ab8 18.♗xa6 ♖xb2 19.♗d3 e4 20.♗xe4 ♖e8 21.♕c4 ♗xe4 22.♕xc7 ♗xf3 23.gxf3 ♕xf3, with a liquidation and a quick draw in Nisipeanu-Svane, Dresden 2017.
17.h3 I was on my own by this stage, but thought this a generally useful waiting move. Now Black has to decide how he wants to set up his pieces.
I notice 17.♕c4 had been played in a couple of earlier games. The position after 17...♕e7 18.♖e1 is rather similar to the game, but I think I get an

improved version as I force Luke's rook to e8 meaning it's trickier to get in ...f7-f5. 18...♔h8 19.♖ad1. This was Vykouk-Haba, Ostrava 2018. Here 19...f5 already looks more pleasant for Black to me.

17...♕e7
This retreat is quite ambitious. If

I don't react, Black is getting ready for ...♔h8 and ...f5. My next couple of moves aim to counter that plan.
18.♖e1 ♖e8 19.♕c4 b5
Double-edged. Black gains a tempo on my queen and opens up the file for his rook, but creates some weaknesses and brings my a1-rook into the game too.

The happy new British Knock-out Champion. Gawain Jones was the only to win a classical game in the championship.

20.axb5 ♖xb5 20...axb5 21.♕b3 ♗e6 22.♖ad1 is slightly more pleasant for White, who can attempt to play on the light squares and exploit the loose b5-pawn.

21.♖ad1!?

21...♖c5?

Black now gets into real difficulties, as his pieces coordinate badly. I'd actually noticed the geometric pattern that finishes the game.

21...♖xb2 was critical, but very dangerous. As Luke was thinking, I was analysing various different sacrifices. The one I was intending was 22.♘xe5 (22.♘g5 ♖f8 doesn't seem to get anywhere) 22...♗xe5 23.♖xe5 ♕xe5 24.♗xf7+ ♔f8 (24...♔h8? runs into back rank issues: 25.♗xe8 ♕xe8 26.♕c7 ♖b7 27.♖d8) 25.♗xe8 ♕xe8 26.♕c5+

ANALYSIS DIAGRAM

and now:

– 26...♔f7 27.♕c7+ ♔g6 is too dangerous for Black: 28.♖d6+ (I'd noticed I had at least a perpetual with 28.♕g3+) 28...♗e6 29.♖xa6. Here the initiative looks too strong.

– 26...♔g8 27.♕a5. The threat of ♖d8 wins back the piece, but the rook and

pawn ending a pawn up shouldn't be enough to win. Best is 27...♖b5! (Black isn't able to hold onto the bishop: 27...♕c6 28.♖d8+ ♔f7 29.♕h5+ ♔e7 30.♕g5+ ♔f7? 31.♕f4+ ♔e7 – or 31...♕f6 32.♕c7+ – 32.♕f8+) 28.♖d8 ♖xa5 29.♖xe8+ ♔f7 30.♖xc8 ♖a1+ 31.♔h2 a5 and Black will successfully trade the a- for the c-pawn leaving a drawn rook and three vs rook and two. 21...♖b4?! doesn't help Black much either. After 22.♕c3, White threatens to take on e5 and so Black has to retreat as 22...a5 23.♗c6 also wins the e-pawn.

22.♕d3 g6 23.c4 a5 Black can't allow White to start rolling his pawns.

24.♕a3

24...♗d6?!

The only way to defend the e5-pawn, but falling into my trap.

Although he has given up professional chess, Luke McShane remains a formidable force. The Englishman could safely call himself one of the strongest amateur players in the world.

My engine suggests Black's best defence would have been 24...♔g7, simply giving up the pawn. However, the ending after 25.♘xe5 ♗xe5 26.♖xe5 ♕xe5 27.♕xc5 ♕xb2 28.♕xa5 is extremely depressing for Black.

25.♗xf7+!

Exploiting Black's vulnerable light squares and clumsy pieces.

25...♕xf7 After 25...♔xf7 26.♖xd6 ♕xd6 27.♘g5+ ♔g7, 28.♘e4 was the slightly hidden point. White wins back the rook and is a pawn up with a dominating position.

26.♖xd6 ♕xc4?!

Now I don't have to show any technique, but Black was already a pawn down and with so many weak squares should just be lost.

27.♘d2!

This retreat ends the game. All Black's major pieces are on their worst possible squares to fight against the knight.

27...♛b4 28.♛xb4 axb4 29.♘e4

Black resigned.

■ ■ ■

Luke McShane gave up professional chess to pursue a career in finance, but when he plays he remains a formidable force. In the semi-final he won the following fine rapid game against England's number one Mickey Adams.

NOTES BY
Luke McShane

Michael Adams
Luke McShane
London British Knockout
Championship 2018 (3.3)
Ruy Lopez, Berlin Defence

1.e4 e5 2.♘f3 ♘c6 3.♗b5 ♘f6
4.0-0 ♘xe4 5.d4 ♘d6 6.♗xc6
dxc6 7.dxe5 ♘f5 8.♛xd8+ ♚xd8
9.h3

9...♗d7

9...♚e8 10.♘c3 h5 is a major battleground in the Berlin lately, including the game between MVL and Nakamura played a few days later.

10.♖d1 ♚c8 11.g4 ♘e7 12.♘g5 ♗e8 13.f4

This brisk mobilisation of the kingside majority is a critical test of Black's setup.

13...h6!?

At Dortmund 2013, the game Caruana-Adams continued 13...h5 14.♚f2 b6 15.f5 ♚b7 16.♘c3 hxg4 17.hxg4 ♖h2+ 18.♚g3 ♖xc2 19.♘h7 c5 20.♘xf8 ♗c6, and with this piece sacrifice Mickey won an energetic game.

Nonetheless, Caruana was happy to repeat the line. In the Super Rapidplay tournament at the 2014 London Chess Classic, he won consecutive White games against David Howell and myself, after 13...f5 14.exf6 gxf6 15.♘e6 ♗d7 16.♘xf8 ♖xf8 17.f5 h5 18.♚f2

ANALYSIS DIAGRAM

and in both games the weak pawn on f6 was the decisive factor.

14.♘f3 f5

An interesting thrust, aiming for an improved version now that the knight has retreated. If memory serves correctly, I had prepared this long before my game against Caruana in 2014, but got the moves mixed up.

15.♚g2 15.exf6 gxf6 is still possible, but White can no longer follow up with ♘g5-e6, so Black keeps the bishop pair in a position which has opened up.

15...♗d7

16.♚g3? I can only guess that Mickey miscalculated or forgot about 16...fxg4 altogether.

16.g5 is ugly, as the pawn majority is comfortably blockaded, but at least White's king is shielded from attack.

16...fxg4! 17.hxg4 h5 18.gxh5 ♖xh5

Black has an easy initiative on the light squares.

19.♘c3 ♖h3+ 20.♔g2 ♗g4 21.♖d3 ♘f5 22.♘g1

22...♘h4+! Surprised at gaining a big edge from the opening, I considered swapping rooks and attacking the weak pawn on d3, but maintaining the attack on the king is far more promising.

23.♔f1 ♖h1 24.♗e3 ♗f5 25.♖d2 ♗e7 26.♔f2

26...♗xc2! The bishop is protected by a skewer. **27.♘ce2 ♖h2+ 28.♔f1 ♘f5 29.♔f2 ♗e4**

30.♘c3 I was hoping for a cheap trick: 30.♖ad1 ♖xf2+ 31.♔xf2 ♗h4+ 32.♔f1 ♘e3 mate.

30...♗g2+ 31.♔e2 b6 32.♘f3 ♖h3 33.♘e1 ♖h1 34.♖ad1 ♗f1+ 35.♔f3 ♔b7

A second rook in the attack proves decisive.

36.♘g2 ♖h3+ 37.♔g4 ♗xg2 38.♔xf5 ♗f3 39.♖d3 ♖f8+ 40.♔e6

On 40.♔g6, 40...♖xf4 wins trivially.

40...♗b4 41.♖g1 ♖h6+ 42.♔d7

42...♗h5

It seems I was determined to honour the 'Berlin bishop', since I didn't notice that 42...♖f7+ is mate in three.

43.♖xg7 ♗e8+ 44.♔d8 ♗f7+ 45.♔d7 ♗e6

Mate. A pretty finish. ∎

NEW IN CHESS bestsellers

Strategic Chess Exercises
Find the Right Way to Outplay Your Opponent
Emmanuel Bricard   224 pages - €24.95

Finally an exercises book that is not about tactics!

"Bricard is clearly a very gifted trainer. He selected a superb range of positions and explains the solutions extremely well." – *Grandmaster Daniel King*

"For chess coaches this book is nothing short of phenomenal." – *Carsten Hansen, author of The Full English Opening*

Winning in the Chess Opening
700 Ways to Ambush Your Opponent
Nikolay Kalinichenko   464 pages - €24.95

More than just a collection of traps and tricks. Kalinichenko always explains the ideas and plans behind the opening and how play could have been improved.

"Enjoyable, while also making the reader much more aware of where early pitfalls can suddenly spring from." *CHESS Magazine*

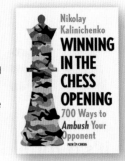

The Full English Opening
Mastering the Fundamentals
Carsten Hansen   464 pages - €29.95

The first one-volume book that covers all variations.

"Currently the best guide in the market. Hansen has clearly put in an amazing amount of work into this book." *IM Kevin Goh Wein Ming*

"A thorough grounding, where the subtleties of the move orders are carefully weighed up, as are the various counters by Black." – *GM Glenn Flear, Yearbook*

Chess Pattern Recognition for Beginners
The Fundamental Guide to Spotting Key Moves in the Middlegame
Arthur van de Oudeweetering   224 pages - €24.95

The author has written two manuals on the subject for advanced players. He now teaches the basics you need to know to develop your pieces, put pressure on your opponent, attack the enemy king, and execute standard sacrifices.

"A great book, which will help every chess player. The examples are very entertaining." – *IM Dirk Schuh*

Strike like Judit!
The Winning Tactics of Chess Legend Judit Polgar
Charles Hertan   256 pages - €24.95

"Thanks to Hertan's well-written explanations, the reader too should be able to increase their own killer instinct." *CHESS Magazine (UK)*

"Judit was a superb tactician, and the book collects her finest combinations."
GM Simen Agdestein, VG Daily Newspaper (Norway)

How Ulf Beats Black
Ulf Andersson's Bulletproof Strategic Repertoire for White
Cyrus Lakdawala   288 pages - €27.95

This repertoire will last a lifetime.

"There is a lot of good stuff to enjoy by exploring the ideas and openings of the Swedish legend."
IM Gary Lane, ECF Newsletter

"Lakdawala has come up with a 'not the usual fare, but definitely worth the detour' type of work. It's instructive, but not too heavy, so will suit all sorts."
GM Glenn Flear, Yearbook 127

Bologan's Caro-Kann
A Modern Repertoire for Black
Victor Bologan   350 pages - €29.95

A complete repertoire that is much more than just a lucidly explained and highly playable set of responses. In many lines Bologan provides two options to handle the Black position. He presents lots of new ideas and resources.

Endgame Virtuoso Magnus Carlsen
His Extraordinary Skills Uncovered and Explained
Tibor Karolyi   272 pages - €24.95

"A real gem!"
GM Karsten Müller, author of 'Fundamental Chess Endings'

"A fantastic book." – *IM Dirk Schuh*

"Karolyi has a pleasant style of analysing: objective, not too many variations, with plenty of diagrams."
IM Hans Bohm, De Telegraaf, NL

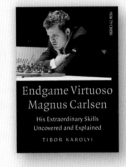

The Fabulous Budapest Gambit
Much more Than Just a Sharp Surprise Weapon
Viktor Moskalenko   288 pages - €27.95

Completely reworked and fully updated from the original 2007 publication; it has been extended by 25% and contains hundreds of improvements, alternatives and new ideas.

"Quite a lot has been changed, including the addition of 50 extra pages, new games and introduction."
Sean Marsh, CHESS Magazine

The Complete French Advance
The Most Uncompromising Way to Attack the French Defence
Evgeny & Vladimir Sveshnikov   288 pages - €29.95

"The author has great experience with this variation and his writings are full of information that any student of the game can learn from." – *GM Glenn Flear*

"A masterclass by the world expert." – *Anatoly Karpov*

"There is plenty of prose explanation and the book is spiced up by exercises to solve and lively observations."
IM John Donaldson

available at your local (chess)bookseller or at www.newinchess.com

Chess Pattern Recognition

ARTHUR VAN DE OUDEWEETERING

Alekhine's Gun

You might also call it the ultimate battery. In any case it's a formidable weapon to have in your arsenal.

o get a feel of what we are talking about, let's warm up with this one:

Alexander Morozevich
Aleksandr Esipenko
Sochi blitz 2017

position after 27...♕f6

In this blitz game, Morozevich had reached a comfortable position and now used the following plan to activate his rooks: **28.♔g2 ♔g7 29.♖h1 ♖h8 30.♗d2 ♗c7 31.h4** After **31...♖ad8?** he soon obtained a winning position, which he converted with enviable restraint. **32.♖h3 ♖h7 33.♕f3 ♖dh8 34.♖ah1 ♗d8 35.♔f1 ♗c7 36.♔e2 ♗d8**

And now, disregarding the tactical shots on g5, Moro quietly played: **37.♖1h2 ♗c7 38.♕h1** 1-0. Indeed an appropriate moment for resignation.

This tripling of major pieces behind your pawn, with the imminent threat of opening the file, is not uncommon. Morozevich's final manoeuvring could have been inspired by this old but equally elegant example.

Vasily Panov
Peter Romanovsky
Moscow 1943

position after 20...♗g7

21.♔g2 ♕c8 22.♖h1 ♗xf5 23.exf5 ♘e7 24.h4 gxh4 Here Black is forced to capture on h4, after which White can direct his forces towards the h7-pawn. **25.♖xh4 ♖f8 26.♗e3 ♖f7 27.♖ah1 ♕g8** 27...♗f8 is refuted by 28.♘xf6 (yes, 28.♖xh7+ also leads to mate, apparently one move earlier) 28...♖xf6 29.♖xh7+ ♔g8 30.♕g4+. **28.♖1h2!** As Panov notes, Black cannot stop the further reinforcement along the h-file. After that, he will be unable to defend both f6 and h7. **28...c6 29.dxc6 ♖c8**

30.♕d1 This queen retreat may already not come as a surprise now, although 30.♔f1, with the idea of ♕f3-h1, a la Moro, might also have been your guess. **30...♗f8 31.c7 ♘c4 32.♗c1 ♖xc7 33.♕h1 ♘d5 34.♗e4 ♘cb6 35.♔g1 ♖fd7 36.♗e3!** Now Black can no longer defend everything. Panov finishes in clean style. **36...♖c5 37.♗xc5 dxc5 38.♗xd5 ♘xd5**

39.♕xd5! White could have done without this simplification, but it is hard to resist. **39...♕xd5 40.♖xh7+ ♖xh7 41.♖xh7+ ♔xh7 42.♘xf6+ ♔h6 43.♘xd5 ♔g5 44.f6 ♗f5 45.♔g2 ♗e6 46.♘c7+ ♔xf6 47.♘xa6 ♗d6 48.♔f3 ♔f5 49.g4+ ♔g5 50.♔e4 ♔xg4 51.♔d5** 1-0.

Now witness the triple battery in a more simplified position.

Irina Krush
Fiona Steil-Antoni
Batumi Olympiad 2018

position after 29...♞a5

30.♕c1! You cannot help loving these subtle backward queen moves. White is going to aim at Black's backward c-pawn. Actually, she had tripled forces on the e-file earlier on, but the e6-pawn could be protected sufficiently. **30...♕f5 31.♖c3 ♖c8 32.♖ec2** The poor thing on c7 is lost. **32...c5 33.bxc6 ♖ec7** and Krush also finished in style:

34.d5!? exd5 35.♔h2 ♕e4 36.f5! ♔g7 37.♖e3 ♕xf5 38.♞d4 ♕g4 39.♞e6+ ♔h7 40.♞xc7 ♖xc7 41.♕e1 ♕xa4 42.♖e7+ ♔h8 43.♖f2 1-0.

This tripling of the major pieces with the rooks in front is known as Alekhine's Gun. Most probably the inspiration for this expression was Alekhine's victory over Nimzowitsch in San Remo 1930, where he finished off his tied-up opponent in

'You cannot help loving these subtle backward queen moves.'

this way along the open c-file. These days there is even a popular video game called Alekhine's Gun. In his comments Alekhine didn't mention the 'Gun' and was more sober. Just like autodidact AlphaZero in the following game.

AlphaZero
Stockfish 8
London Computer Match 2018

position after 31...♔g8

Having abandoned the c-file at an earlier stage, Stockfish must have felt as helpless as Nimzowitsch, also because Alpha Zero has a second front available on the kingside. **32.♖c2 ♗c8** 32...♖c8 33.♖ec1 ♖xc2 34.♕xc2 and the c-file is White's. **33.♕c1 ♗a6 34.♖d1 ♔h8 35.♖c6 ♗e2 36.♖d2 ♗xf3+ 37.♔xf3 ♕e8 38.♖dc2**

And that's that. **38...♞b6 39.♖c7 ♞c4** Do I discern some human despair here? **40.bxc4** and, seven moves later, 1-0.

Alekhine's Gun is also a familiar weapon to besiege an isolated central pawn. In my book *Train Your Chess Pattern Recognition* you may find the instructive Karpov-Spassky game from Montreal 1979. Here is another effective example.

Marc Esserman
Giorgi Kacheishvili
Charlotte 2011

position after 26.♕c3

26...♖d6 27.♖e4 ♖bd8 28.g4 ♖8d7 29.h3 ♕d8

Well, that was quick. Meanwhile White has prevented ...♞e7-f5, but that comes with an obvious drawback. **30.♖a5 g5!** The hasty 30...♖xd4? 31.♖xd4 ♖xd4 32.♖xa7 would spoil the advantage. **31.♖a6 ♞g6 32.♗a4 ♖xd4 33.♖xd4 ♖xd4 34.♖xa7?** This loses on the spot. But 34.♖xc6 ♞f4! would still have left Black with a huge advantage. **34...♖xa4!** 0-1.

So, if you're looking for ways to put pressure on your opponent, do not forget that one of the weapons you should be carrying is Alekhine's Gun! ∎

Ju Wenjun remains Women's World Champion

The background story of her title defence told by her coach

As Ju Wenjun was fighting in Khanty-Mansiysk to keep her title, she could always rely on her trainer Ni Hua back home in Shanghai. Every day the Women's World Champion would speak seven to eight hours(!) with the experienced GM, who was a member of the golden Chinese team that won the 2014 Olympiad. Allowing us a peek behind the scenes, **NI HUA** looks back on three long weeks of chess and comments on the key games of the final of the knockout championship.

Ju Wenjun and I are good friends and have been on friendly terms for many years. We both work in the Chess and Cards Games Administration Centre in Shanghai as government employees. Besides chess, we have Go, Chinese chess, draughts, checkers and Five Chess, in total six games. Go is the most popular mind game in China, more so than chess, but our chess team has achieved the best results for our centre. Our team consists of some 10 people, including a coach and a captain. We play in the Chinese Chess League and we have regular training sessions, during which we work on hard puzzles and play rapid games, with the losers having to buy afternoon tea.

Ju Wenjun and I have represented the team for 14 years now. Six times we won the national championship. Our centre is located on the prosperous West Nanjing Road. It used to be a very small place, but a few years ago a new building was constructed on the old location. We have our own canteen, a world-class playing hall, a training area and a chess and cards museum. Chess lovers from all over the world are welcome to visit.

Like a top male player

Still, my work with Ju Wenjun only started in 2016, after the Baku Olympiad, when she needed to win the last leg of the Grand Prix to obtain the right to challenge the World Champion, Tan Zhongyi. My approach has been to require her to train like a top male player and she has accomplished a 'mission impossible' with great endurance. During the past two years, she has won the World Championship, twice, the Rapid World Championship, and an Olympiad gold medal. These good results are the best reward for her hard work.

Ju Wenjun is tough, she can endure loneliness, and she is very keen on chess. She longs for victory, and although I could feel she was a bit nervous in the match against Tan, she nevertheless prevailed. At the last Olympiad and in Khanty-Mansiysk, she showed the confidence of a World Champion. I was not surprised by her victory, even though she was trailing at some point.

The fact that Ju Wenjun had to take part in the knock-out championship means that the reigning champion has no privileges at all. It's a problem that has been solved by the new FIDE leadership for the next cycle, when there will be a Candidates tournament, but for her there was no choice but stick to the rules and travel to Siberia. Because we were confident that she could fight for the title (note that I write 'fight for the title' and not 'defend her title'), even though the knock-out system is unpredictable, she needed to be in the right frame of mind and she was. She proceeded

World Champion Ju Wenjun together with FIDE president Arkady Dvorkovich and runner-up Kateryna Lagno at the prize-giving in Khanty-Mansiysk.

confidently without having to play any tiebreaks. This saved her a lot of energy for her final spurt.

Oreo cookies

The Chinese delegation included a coach, Yu Shaoteng, and an interpreter. The players who got eliminated didn't stay around to help the others, but went back to China immediately. The interpreter could help Ju Wenjun to buy things from the supermarket, but as regards technical chess matters she only communicated with me. In a way she was all alone in Khanty-Mansiysk. Her friends and family could only cheer her up through internet communication.

Of late she has started to bring lots of Oreo cookies to tournaments, but I think her most important talisman was the support from her family, the people at the Shanghai office and her coach.

There was a three-hour time difference between Khanty-Mansiysk and Shanghai. I would speak with her after her game until two or three am my time. In the morning we would continue to work. We talked to each other seven or eight hours a day, especially after the semi-final. This does not include the time I spent to prepare for the game. During the match I spent a lot of time looking at the computer. After the match had finished, I went out and my eyes felt extremely uncomfortable; a clear sign of too much screen and too little sunshine.

She never gives up

The crucial moment in the match was, of course, the final. As Ju Wenjun had not played any tie-breaks, it was easier for her, because her opponent

'In a way Ju Wenjun was all alone in Khanty-Mansiysk.'

Kateryna Lagno had gone through several. However, Kateryna caused her serious trouble. Her strength and confidence were so different from the other competitors. It was for exactly that reason that I had always believed that Kateryna had the biggest chance to reach the final.

In the second game of the final, Lagno showed her exquisite endgame technique to win the game. In the third round, we prepared really well and got a huge advantage, but failed to win. In the last round of the classical part, Ju Wenjun had to win. That was tough, but again she showed that she never gives up. We chose the right opening to lead the game into unpredictable territory and she ended up winning.

Let's take a look at those two games, which to my mind were the decisive moments in the championship.

NOTES BY
Ni Hua

Ju Wenjun
Kateryna Lagno
Khanty-Mansiysk 2018 (6.3)
King's Indian Defence

After the first two rounds of the four-game final, Ju Wenjun was trailing ½-1½ and needed to catch up. This would be her last game with White in the classical games, and we had pinned our hopes on this one.

Lagno has played the Grünfeld against 1.d4 all through her career, but in the first game of the final she went for the King's Indian. Both players fought hard in a not very popular line, both of them missed opportunities and the game ended in a draw.

For this round we had mainly prepared the KID, hoping to surprise our opponent a bit.

1.d4 ♘f6 2.c4 g6 3.♘c3 ♗g7 4.e4 In the first game, Ju Wenjun chose the more solid 4.g3.

4...d6 5.♗d3

We believed that her opponent would not be very experienced in this line. Let's just wait and see how she's going to deal with it.

5...0-0 6.♘ge2 c5

The alternative is 6...♘c6 7.0-0 e5 8.d5 ♘d4, which might be more solid. But Lagno prefers to push ...c5 in such positions.

7.d5 e6 8.♗g5!?

This leads to an intense fight.

White can also decide to go 8.h3 or 8.0-0, but if you are trying to win, it is necessary to avoid ...exd5 exd5, with a symmetrical position.

8...h6 9.♗h4 exd5

Here both Ding Liren and Grischuk played 9...g5 10.♗g3 ♘h5, which I do not believe to be a safe and reliable continuation.

10.♘xd5 g5

Black might consider 10...♘c6 instead, which will be safe enough, although the d6-pawn will become a permanent weakness. White would be slightly better, but Black is fine.

11.♗g3 ♘xd5 12.cxd5 ♗xb2 13.h4

13...g4

There was no need to worry about 13...♗xa1, as it was part of our home

preparation: 14.♕xa1 g4 15.0-0 f5 (or 15...♖e8 16.♗f4) 16.e5, and I would prefer White.

14.♖b1 ♗g7 15.0-0 ♖e8

So far everything was still our home preparation. I have to say that this is a pleasant position for White. White has sacrificed a pawn for quicker development, Black's king is potentially weak, and Lagno was unfamiliar with this position, which is always a very good thing. What more could Ju Wenjun have wanted?

16.♘f4 c4?

Perhaps a better option was 16...♘d7, but then Black's position is very dangerous after 17.♘h5. Even the best strategic player would panic when his or her king is under such an attack.

17.♗xc4 ♖xe4

18.♗d3

Here 18.♕c2 would have given White an even fiercer attack: 18...♖e5 19.♘e6! fxe6 20.♗xe5 dxe5 21.dxe6, and White should be winning. After 18...♖e8, 19.♘h5 is strong.

18...♖e5 19.f3 h5 20.♗e2 ♕d7

White is also clearly better after 20...♘d7 21.fxg4 hxg4 22.♗xg4.

21.♖b4

Ju Wenjun did not spend much time on this move. Her intention was to exchange the rooks with ♖e4 and grab the h5-pawn. But she missed an excellent chance to knock out her opponent: 21.fxg4 hxg4 22.♘e6!!, with a mating attack: 22...fxe6 23.♗xe5 ♗xe5 (or 23...dxe5 24.♗xg4, and wins) 24.♗c4, and Black is lost.

21...♘a6 22.♖e4 ♖xe4 23.fxe4 ♘c5 24.e5!

Blocking Black's g7-bishop and supporting White's d5-pawn at the same time.

24...dxe5 25.♘xh5 ♘e4

26.♗e1

This is a bit slow and gives her opponent a chance to breathe.

Better was 26.d6, to maintain the pressure. For example: 26...♕xd6 27.♕xd6 ♘xd6 28.♘xg7 ♔xg7 29.♗xe5+, and Black is lost. Or 26...♕c6 27.♗xg4 (27.♘xg7 would lose to 27...♘xg3) 27...♕xd6 28.♕xd6 ♘xd6 29.♗xc8 ♘xc8 30.♘xg7 ♔xg7 31.♗xe5+ ♔g8 32.♖f3, and Black is in deep trouble.

26...f5 27.♘xg7 ♕xg7 28.♗d3

28...♗d7?

The move called for was 28...♘d6. After the knight retreat Black's structure is solid, and she finishes the development of her pieces, which is a huge step forward.

29.♗xe4 fxe4 30.♗g3 ♖f8 31.♖e1 ♗b5 32.♕b3 ♗d3 33.d6+ ♕f7 34.♕c3 ♕e6

35.♕xe5

Although 35.♕c7 would keep the queens on the board, it would have been a better move. Ju Wenjun said

Ni Hua did accompany Ju Wenjun to St. Petersburg, where at the King Salman Rapid & Blitz World Championships, she also added the rapid world title to her collection.

that she couldn't see a clear attack, and felt that the text-move would give White easier play that should be enough to win the endgame.

35...♕xe5 36.♗xe5 ♔f7 37.g3 ♔e6 38.♗f4 b5 39.h5 a5

40.h6? The last move before the time-control, which is always a crucial moment. White really needed to block e3 with the king, so that when Black played ...e3, she wouldn't need to waste the move ♗xe3 to take the pawn. Moreover, the rook needs to go out via c1, and the h-pawn is in no rush to advance. These details should be the key points for this

endgame. Here are the lines: 40.♔f2 b4 41.♖c1 a4 42.♖c7

ANALYSIS DIAGRAM

and now 42...b3 43.axb3 axb3 44.♖b7, and White wins. Or 42...♖f7 43.♖xf7 ♔xf7 44.♗d2 b3 45.axb3 axb3 46.♗c1 ♔e6 (White also wins after 46...♗b5 47.♔e3 ♗c6 48.♔d4 ♔g7 49.h6+ ♔h7 50.♔c3 ♗a4 51.♔b2 ♔g6 52.♔a3) 47.♔e3, winning.

40...b4 41.♖c1 a4 42.♖c7 b3 43.axb3 axb3

44.♖e7+

After 44.♖b7, 44...e3! is the key move: 45.♗xe3 ♖f1+ 46.♔g2 ♖e1 47.d7 ♖xe3 48.d8♕ ♖e2+ 49.♔f1 ♖e3+, with a draw.

44...♔d5 45.♖b7

45...e3?

After 45...♔c4, Black must play accurately to draw. White may get a queen, but cannot achieve much. Still, it would be hard to find all this in a real game: 46.♔f2 e3+

47.♔xe3 ♖e8+ 48.♔d2 b2 49.d7 ♖e2+ 50.♔d1 ♖e7 51.d8♕ ♖xb7 52.♕c8+ ♔d4 53.♕h8+ ♔e4 54.♕e5+ ♔f3 55.♕d5+ ♔e4, and after the capture on b7 this should be a draw.

46.♖xb3 ♔e4

47.♔g2!

The only winning move. In case of 47.♖b7 Black has excellent drawing chances: 47...♔f3!! 48.h7 ♖c8 49.♖c7 ♖b8 50.♗e5 ♖b1+ 51.♔h2 ♖d1! 52.♖f7+ ♔e2 53.♖a7 (and not

53.h8♕ ♗e4! and Black wins!), with a draw.

47...e2

48.♖b4+?

Missing the win. She should have played 48.♖b7, after which the variations go as follows: 48...e1♘+ (the only move) 49.♔f2 ♘f3 50.♖e7+ ♔f5 51.h7 ♖a8 52.♗c1 (and not 52.d7 ♗b5 53.♖e8 ♖a2+ 54.♔e3 ♖e2 mate) 52...♘g5 (52...♗b5 loses to 53.♗b2) 53.♗xg5 ♔xg5 54.d7 ♗xh7 55.♖e8 ♖a2+ 56.♔e1 ♖a1+ 57.♔d2 ♖a2+

58.♔c1 ♖a1+ 59.♔b2 ♖b1+ 60.♔c3 ♖d1 61.d8♕+ ♖xd8 62.♖xd8, and White wins.

48...♔d5 49.♔f2 ♖e8 50.♗d2 ♖f8+! The simplest way to draw.

51.♗f4

Since 51.♔e3 ♖f3 is mate, and neither 51.♔g2 ♗e4+ nor 51.♔g1 ♗e4 are advisable.

White has no way to make progress except for 51.♖f4, but after the rook swap her king cannot move freely, as it has to cling to the black pawn on e2.

51...♖e8 52.♗d2 ♖f8+ 53.♖f4 ♖xf4+ 54.♗xf4 ♔e6 55.♗e1 ♔d7 56.♗e5 ♔e6 57.♔d2 ♔d7 58.♗c3

58...e1♕+!

Without this move White's bishop would get to b4, but now there is no such thing.

59.♔xe1 ♔xd6 60.♔d2 ♗h7 61.♔e3 ♔e6 62.♔f4 ♔f7 63.♔xg4 ♗c2 64.♔f4 ♗b1 65.g4 ♗c2 66.g5 ♗b1 67.♔e5 ♗c2 68.♔d6 ♗b1

Draw.

NOTES BY
Ni Hua

**Kateryna Lagno
Ju Wenjun**
Khanty-Mansiysk 2018 (6.4)
Sicilian Defence, Rossolimo Variation

That she failed to win Game 3 was a clear disappointment for Ju Wenjun. After the game she told me that she had been too tired. Luckily, before the fourth and last classical game she still kept believing that she could equal the score. But she felt extra pressure because of the missed chances.

1.e4

Lagno went for 1.♘f3 in the second game, and managed to transpose to a popular line of the Catalan. She

A salute to the World Champion's team! This is the system that Magnus

system and Caruana used it in the men's World Champion match, but if Lagno wanted to make a draw, there would have been safer choices.

3...g6 4.0-0 ♗g7 5.♖e1 e5!

> ## 'Lagno is an all-rounder and played very solidly. It is quite hard to drag her into a complicated battle.'

showed her strong endgame technique to win the game in text-book style. However, 1.♘f3 is not her main weapon and because a draw in the last round would be enough for her to win the title, we had focused more on a king's pawn opening in our preparation.

1...c5 2.♘f3 ♘c6 3.♗b5

The Rossolimo Variation. It is hard to condemn this move, since it is practically the best move against the ...♘c6

Carlsen played in the first few games of the World Championship match in London. Needless to say, both teams in that match have studied this system deeply. For us, it was pretty much for lack of other choices.

6.a3

Here Caruana played 6.b4, while the alternative is 6.♗xc6, which is also quite nice. To be honest, we felt satisfied to be able to fight in a middle-game like this.

6...♘ge7 7.♘c3 0-0 8.♗c4 d6 9.d3 h6 10.♘d5 ♔h7 11.c3

Here White could have pushed 11.b4 immediately. I need to mention that we had prepared a similar position in which White didn't play ♖e1 and c3. Psychologically, Ju Wenjun could be content. Lagno played this game too carefully and a bit haphazardly. Her performance in this game seemed like that of a completely different person compared to the rest of the Championship.

11...f5! In this semi-closed position, Black starts attacking the white king and White doesn't look like getting anywhere on the queenside. ♖e1 and c3 are two wasted tempi, according to our home preparation, so why not ...f5?
12.exf5 gxf5

13.b4 Here, White had a tactical means to stop Black's pieces gathering on the kingside: 13.♘g5+ ♔g6 14.♘xe7+ ♕xe7 15.♘h3 ♔h7 16.♘f4, which would have been much better than the game.
13...♘g6 Black is already better.
14.b5?! ♘a5

Now Black can energetically move all her pieces to reinforce the kingside attack.

15.♗a2 ♗e6 16.♕a4?! b6 17.♗d2 ♖g8 18.♖ad1 ♕d7 19.♘h4

19...♖h8 White's 14.b5 and 16.♕a4 were not the best moves. Blocking the knight on the queenside with b5 would be a good choice in some positions in the English Opening, but there Black does not have the chance to attack the king.
Now the knight on a5 can be helpful, and in fact, 19...c4! would have won immediately: 20.♘xg6 ♗xd5 21.dxc4 ♗e6 22.♘h4 ♗f6 23.♘f3 ♕b7, and White's position will soon collapse.
20.♘xg6 ♖xg6 21.♕h4 ♖ag8 22.g3 ♕f7 23.c4

23...♗f6? From a practical point of view, this move yielded a good result, but objectively speaking it is not a good move. Here she should have pushed 23...f4! at once, for example: 24.♗xa5 ♗f6 25.♘xf6+ ♖xf6 26.♗c3 ♖g4, and game over.
24.♘xf6+ ♖xf6 25.f4 ♖g4 26.♕h3 ♖fg6 27.♖f1
Better was 27.♕f1 ♕f6 28.♖e2 ♗c8, although Black keeps the initiative.
27...♕g7

28.♔h1??
A blunder! Here the only way for White to defend against Black's attack on the g-file was 28.♕h5!, as Black cannot play 28...♖xg3+ 29.hxg3 ♖xg3+ in view of 30.♔h2 ♖g2+ 31.♔h1, so Black will have to slow down and try to build up more pressure.
28...♗c8! Including the other bishop into the attack. White's bishop pair is useless. There is no way to save the game anymore.
29.♕h5 ♗b7+ 30.♔g1

30...♖xg3+ 31.hxg3 ♖xg3+ 32.♔f2 ♖g2+ White resigned.
This victory brought about a big change for both players. Suddenly they had traded tiredness and the psychological advantage. After this game Ju Wenjun told me that she didn't feel tired anymore. Lagno, on the other hand, had already played several play-offs on her way to the final, and not being able to avoid another play-off must have been tough on her. However, I still think she deserves all the praise and honour, and it would have been absolutely appropriate if she had won the match. ■

MAXIMize
your Tactics
with Maxim Notkin

Find the best move in the positions below

Solutions on page 105

1. Black to play

2. White to play

3. White to play

4. White to play

5. Black to play

6. Black to play

7. White to play

8. White to play

9. Black to play

Chuky's waiting move: Surprises on move 4 in the English Four Knights

Jeroen Bosch

In the game Ivanchuk-Paravyan, Batumi 2018, the Ukrainian genius played 4.h3!? in an English Four Knights and duly won. This result was perhaps not directly linked to 4.h3, but it did make me wonder why Ivanchuk would make such an insipid move. As an added bonus, I will mention a few other SOS-possibilities on move 4 as well.

1.c4 e5 2.♘c3 ♘f6 3.♘f3 ♘c6 4.h3!?

This looks odd, and indeed it is! To discover the 'method behind the madness' we need to observe how Black replies to the main line moves 4.g3 and 4.e3.

■ By far the most popular move is 4.g3. For our purposes it is sufficient to know that Black has the following options:

– to go for a reversed Sicilian Dragon with 4...d5.
– to play 4...♗b4 (a reversed Rossolimo Sicilian if you like!).

The problem for White is that the tempting 5.♘d5 (5.♗g2 is, of course, the main line) can be met by 5...♘xd5 6.cxd5 ♘d4, and now taking the pawn with 7.♘xe5? fails to 7...♕e7!, but White keeps a slight edge with 7.♘xd4 exd4 8.♕c2, as played in Kortchnoi-Karpov, Baguio City 1978. In reply to 5.♘d5, Black has other decent replies as well, e.g. 5...e4!? and 5...♗c5.
– Finally, after 4...♗c5 the pseudo-sacrifice 5.♘xe5 is not particularly strong in view of 5...♗xf2+ 6.♔xf2 ♘xe5 7.e4 c5, when Black controls some important dark squares.

■ The other main line is 4.e3, and this move renders the reversed Open Sicilian with 4...d5 unattractive because of 5.cxd5 ♘xd5 6.♗b5! However, the Rossolimo reply 4...♗b4! is fine, and the main line starting with 5.♕c2 is currently very fashionable in 2700- and 2800-circles. For us it is useful to know that 5.♘d5 (a move that looks tempting) can be met by 5...e4! 6.♘g1 0-0, when Black is fine, since White had to 'undevelop' his king's knight.

For the purposes of this article, I will not go into 4.d4 and 4.e4. However, before we move on to Ivanchuk's 4.h3 I would like to mention a few other possibilities:
■ Certainly not the least of these options is moving the other rook pawn with 4.a3!? Obviously, White prevents 4...♗b4 (which, as we have

'This looks odd, and indeed it is!'

seen, is Black's main reply after both 4.g3 and 4.e3), and after 4...d5 5.cxd5 ♘xd5 we have, of course, an open Sicilian with colours reversed in which Black (White) has the useful extra move ...a6. All strong players now continue with the typical Sicilian queen move 6.♕c2!?.

This has been played by Carlsen and Caruana, but also by many other great players. One of the most recent top-level games is Topalov-Giri, Shamkir 2018.

Unlike 4.h3, 4.a3 has been played in thousands of games, but this should not necessarily deter you. Here are two pieces of advice:

1. If you can get hold of an old copy of SOS-3 (New In Chess, 2005), study the chapter written by Mikhail Gurevich.

2. Study the games of the specialists Alex Chernin and Mikhail Gurevich.

■ Another, less theoretical option is 4.d3, although with this move, too, you will find thousands of games in your database. It's simply a decent move, and not very critical.

– Black either goes for an open Sicilian again with 4...d5 5.cxd5 ♘xd5, when

White faces a choice between a Scheve-ningen set-up with 6.e3, a Dragon set-up with 6.g3, and the 'Sveshnikov' move 6.e4!?.

– The other main option after 4.d3 is once again 4...♗b4.

Finally, I would like to mention two queen moves that are hardly ever played:

■ A move that easily falls within the SOS concept is the surprising 4.♕a4!? (Murey).

What I like about this move is that it prevents Black's customary 4th-move replies in the English Four Knights.

Thus, 4...d5?! is obviously bad due to 5.cxd5 ♘xd5 6.♘xe5±, and 4...♗b4?! is met by 5.♘xe5! ♗xc3 6.♘xc6 ♗xd2+ 7.♗xd2 dxc6 8.♖d1.

Sensible replies are 4...♗e7 and 4...♗c5, and so is 4...g6.

■ If you are willing to consider the SOS move 4.♕a4, you should also look at the sharp 4...e4, which leads to interesting play after 5.♘g5 ♕e7 and now either 6.f3 exf3 7.♘xf3, or 6.c5!?.

■ Less odd is the other queen move 4.♕c2!? which, however, does not prevent 4...♗b4 or 4...d5.

A few sample lines should give you an inkling of what is going on:

– 4...♗e7 5.e3 0-0 6.a3 d5 7.cxd5 ♘xd5 8.b4 ♘xc3 9.dxc3 ♕d6 10.♗d3 f5 11.e4 f4 12.h3 a5 13.♗b2 ♗f6 was Carlsen-Bu Xiangzhi, Riyadh rapid 2017. White is a bit better at this stage.

– 4...♗b4 5.♘d5 (5.e3 transposes to a popular main line) 5...0-0 6.a3 (6.e3) 6...♗c5 7.e3 a5, Sadek-Aly, Assiut 2009, and now 8.♘g5 (8.♗d3!?) 8...g6 9.♘xf6+ (9.h4!?) 9...♕xf6 10.♘e4 ♕e7 11.b3 looks somewhat better for White.

– 4...g6, and now something sensible like 5.a3 a5 6.e3 ♗g7 7.♗e2 0-0 8.0-0, as in Kunte-Roy Chowdhury, New Delhi 2001, should be equal.

– Black has not tried 4...d4 5.♘xd4 exd4 6.♘d5 in practice.

– 4...d5 5.cxd5 ♘xd5 6.♘xe5!? (6.a3; 6.e3 ♘xc3 7.bxc3 ♗d6) 6...♘xe5 7.♕e4, Zalys-Ledain, Montreal 1957, and White won a pawn, but Black has sufficient compensation in view of his edge in development after 7...♗d6 and castling.

We are now fully equipped to look at Ivanchuk's 4.h3!?. His opponent now went:

4...a6!? The bloody cheek! Black does not in any way try to take advantage of the odd 4.h3, but simply returns the move to White.

■ As we know, 4...♗b4 needs to be investigated:

– Practice has seen 5.♕c2 0-0 6.♘d5 ♗d6, as in Hassim-Malmström, LSS email 2009. However, I am not that taken with 5.♕c2, because when Black plays 6...♖e8!, we have ended up in a theoretical position from the 4.e3-line in which White normally has a pawn on e3 and his h-pawn on the original square. This is clearly much better for White, so we should discard 5.♕c2.

Whether good or bad, only two moves have some logic after White has played 4.h3. One idea behind 4.h3 could be that after 4...♗b4 White can play – 5.♘d5!?, because after 5...e4 the knight is no longer forced to retreat to the first rank, but has an unlikely square available in the form of 6.♘h2!?.

One plausible line is 6...0-0 7.a3 ♗e7 8.d3 exd3 9.e3 ♘e5 10.♗xd3 ♘xd3+ 11.♕xd3, and Black's bishop pair and White's space advantage result in a more or less equal game.

Instead, strange complications may result from 6...♘xd5 7.cxd5 ♘e7 8.a3 ♗d6 9.d3 ♘xd5 (9...e3!? 10.♗xe3 ♘xd5 11.♗d2 ♗xh2!? 12.♖xh2 0-0 is structurally better for White, but the rook looks very silly on h2, of course) 10.dxe4 ♘f6 11.♕d4 ♕e7 12.♘g4!

and now 12...♘xe4 (12...h5 13.♘xf6+ ♕xf6 14.♕xf6 gxf6 15.g3 is an amusing endgame) 13.♕xg7 ♗b4+ 14.axb4 ♕xb4+ 15.♔d1 ♕b3+ 16.♔e1 ♕b4+ is a crazy drawing line.
– The only other consistent move (like it or not) is 5.g4!?, when the plausible sequence 5...0-0 6.♗g2 e4 7.♘h2 (yes, 4.h3 had a point!) 7...♖e8 8.0-0

leads to a kind of 'extended version' of

the 4.g3 main line. The knight on h2 will get back into the game after some time (g5 and ♘g4, f3 and taking back on f3, or f4). We are, of course, in utterly virgin territory.

■ I guess that the most consistent reply to 4...d5 is 5.cxd5 ♘xd5, and now 6.e4, when the extra h3 (...h6 in the Sicilian Sveshnikov) is at least useful in preventing ...♗g4 to cement Black's control of square d4.

Let's first note that 6...♘xc3 7.bxc3 is pleasant for White, while 6...♘b6 is met by 7.♗b5, as is 6...♘f6 7.♗b5!. So Black faces the following choice:
– To play 6...♘f4 7.d4 exd4 8.♗xf4 dxc3 9.bxc3 ♕f6 10.♕d2 and in the Sveshnikov White (so here Black) now plays ♗g5 (...♗g4 here which is obviously not on). The game is nevertheless equal.
– Or to go 6...♘db4, as in the Sveshnikov. After 7.d3 there is no ...♗g4, so Black may opt for 7...♘d4 (7...a5) 8.♘xd4 exd4, when the main line with reversed colours goes 9.♘b1 c5 10.♗e2 ♗d6 11.0-0 0-0 12.a3 ♘c6 13.f4 f6 14.♗g4.

Let's not kid ourselves. Objectively, the extra move h3 means nothing here, yet the position is sufficiently interesting, and we have most likely shocked our

opponent by playing the Sveshnikov with White!
■ Let's note that 4...♗c5 is met by 5.♘xe5! ♗xf2+ (5...♘xe5 6.d4±) 6.♔xf2 ♘xe5, and compared to 4.g3 ♗c5 5.♘xe5 it is pretty favourable for White to have a pawn on h3 (rather than on g3). Thus square g4 is covered from annoying checks and White should be better and might like to continue energetically with the pawn sac 7.d4!? (7.e3) 7...♘xc4 8.e4! d5 9.e5.
■ 4...e4 5.♘g5 ♕e7 actually also exists with reversed colours (1.e4 c5 2.♘f3 ♘c6 3.♘c3 ♘f6 4.e5?! ♘g4 5.♕e2). Here the h-pawn has been moved one square. 6.d3 (6.♕c2 leads to much sharper play) 6...exd3 7.e3 ♕c5 (7...♘b4 8.♗xd3 ♘xd3+ 9.♕xd3, and despite Black's bishop pair, White is slightly better) 8.e4

and in the theoretical Sicilian position (so with reversed colours and without the additional h2-h3) they now play 8...h6, when 9.♘f3 is unplayable in view of 9...♘g4 – a very deep line to prove the value of 4.h3...!

Because of the 'insipid' nature of 4.h3 there is nothing wrong with any of the more restrained options that Black has on move 4.
■ After 4...g6 play could continue 5.e3 ♗g7 6.d4 exd4 7.exd4 d5 8.♗d3 0-0 9.0-0, when the pawn on h3 is at least very useful in preventing ...♗g4.
■ In case of 4...♗e7 it is interesting to play 5.g4!? (also possible is 5.d3 d5 6.cxd5 ♘xd5 7.e4) 5...0-0 (5...e4 6.♘h2 6.♘g5 h5! – 6...0-0 7.♗g2) 6.d3.
■ 4...d6 can be met by 5.e3 and a future d4, or by the immediate 5.d4.
■ If Black really wanted to preserve the status quo (as Ivanchuk's opponent did with 4...a6), I would have done so with

the waiting move 4...h6!?. ...h7-h6 is often useful in these English positions to take away square g5 from White's bishop or knight. Indeed, 1.c4 e5 2.g3 ♘f6 3.♗g2 h6!? is a respectable line played by Anand and Carlsen (versus Kramnik in the 2011 Tal Memorial).

Ivanchuk now went **5.e3** after which Black demonstrated the usefulness of his rook pawn move by playing **5...d5**. Note that White meets 5...♗b4 with 6.♘d5. Black's idea is that after 5...d5 6.cxd5 ♘xd5 Black's a6 is more useful than White's h3.

6.d4! Aiming for a type of position in which h3 is a useful addition.

6...exd4 Or 6...dxc4 7.♗xc4 exd4 8.exd4 ♗d6 9.0-0 0-0.

This is a position that can also arise from the French Exchange and from the Queen's Gambit Accepted. White is a bit better after 10.♗g5 h6 11.♗h4 ♗f5 (11...♖e8 12.♕b3; 11...♗e7 12.♖e1; 11...g5 12.♘xg5! hxg5 13.♗xg5 ♗e7 14.♖e1) 12.♖e1. Things now went worse after 12...♘b4?! 13.♖e2 b5 14.♗b3 c5? 15.dxc5 ♗xc5 16.♘d2 (16.♕xd8 ♖fxd8 17.♖e5 also wins) 16...♕b8 17.♗xf6 gxf6 18.a3 ♘c6 19.♖d5 ♖d8 20.♕c1 ♖xd5 21.♘xd5 1-0, Kosashvili-Visser, Netherlands 2002.

7.exd4 ♗b4 8.♗d3 dxc4 9.♗xc4 0-0 10.0-0

10...♗f5 Via other move orders the following games have been played:
– 10...h6 11.♗e3 (11.a3 ♗d6 12.♖e1) 11...♗d6, Georgescu-Bauer, London 2015, and now 12.♕c1 with sacrificial thoughts in mind: 12...b5 (12...♖e8 13.♗xh6!; 12...♗f5 13.♗xh6!? gxh6 14.♕xh6, with decent compensation) 13.♗d3 ♘b4 14.♗b1 ♖e8, and now 15.a3 ♘bd5 16.♘xd5 ♘xd5 17.♗xh6 gxh6 18.♕xh6 only leads to a draw after 18...♕f6 19.♗h7+ ♔h8 20.♗g6+.
– 10...b5 11.♗b3 (11.♗d3) 11...♗f5 12.♗g5 h6?! 13.♗xf6 ♕xf6 14.♘d5 ♕d6, De Strycker-Filipovic, Pula 2017, and now 15.♘e5! is strong.

11.a3 ♗d6 Perhaps 11...♗xc3 12.bxc3 ♘e4 13.♗b2 b5 to try for a light-square blockade.

12.♗g5 h6 13.♗h4 g5 White is better after 13...♖e8?! 14.♕d2!, intending 14...g5?? (14...♗e7 15.♖ae1±) 15.♘xg5. White also keeps an edge after 13...♗e7 14.♗g3 or 14.♖e1.

14.♗g3 14.♘xg5 hxg5 15.♗xg5, with compensation but nothing decisive.

14...♘e4?! 14...♗xg3 15.fxg3; 14...♖e8 15.♕b3 ♗g6 16.♘e5.

15.♘xe4 ♗xe4 16.♘e5

White has a clear initiative now.

16...♗xe5 Black – with his weakened kingside – loses after 16...♘xe5 17.dxe5 ♗e7 18.♕g4 ♗g6 19.♖ad1.

17.dxe5 ♕e7
17...♕xd1 18.♖axd1, followed by f4, is also good for White.

18.♕e1!? ♗f5 **19.♕c3** Even stronger are 19.♕e3 and 19.♖c1.

19...♖ad8 20.b4 20.f4 was another option. Black has counterplay after 20.♗xa6 ♘d4 21.♖ad1 c5.

20...♗e6? 21.♗xa6! Now that Black can no longer support the knight on d4 with ...c5, this is strong.

21...♘d4 21...bxa6 22.♕xc6, and White not only has an extra pawn, but Black's weakened kingside may also play a role in the conversion of White's advantage. Nevertheless, this was perhaps Black's best chance.

22.♖ad1 ♕d7 23.♗d3 ♗b3 24.♖d2 ♗a4?
More tenacious was 24...♘e2+ 25.♖xe2 ♕xd3 26.♖e3 ♕xc3 27.♖xc3 ♗e6 28.♖xc7 b5.

25.♖e1 25.♗c4!. **25...♗c6 26.♖ed1 ♕d5 27.f3 ♕e6 28.♗c4**

White is completely winning. The final moves were **28...♘b5 29.♕b3 ♖xd2 30.♗xe6 ♖d1+ 31.♕xd1 fxe6 32.a4 ♘a7 33.♕c2 ♔g7 34.b5 ♗d5 35.♕xc7+ ♔g6 36.♗f2** 1-0, Ivanchuk-Paravyan, Batumi 2018.

In conclusion, if you are willing to experiment: start the game with 4.h3 and proceed into the 'unknown'. If 4.h3 feels like stretching things a bit too far, then 4.♕a4 and 4.♕c2 are options as well, and finally there are 4.a3 and 4.d3 to consider as less theoretical alternatives for the main lines 4.g3 and 4.e3. ■

Speeding Up

Is it an insult to our age-old pursuit to decide the World Championship match in a rapid tiebreaker or is it only natural in our faster modern times? **MAXIM DLUGY** didn't understand the commotion in the wake of the Carlsen-Caruana match and sees faster play as a blessing for the future of chess.

As we witnessed a second World Championship match in a row decided by a rapid tiebreaker – first Carlsen-Karjakin in New York, now Carlsen-Caruana in London – thousands of people started discussing the possibility of changing the format of the World Chess Championship match. The gist of their objections was that sponsors cannot possibly be happy with 12 draws followed by random fast-paced chess moves to determine the eventual winner.

It has been becoming clear over the last 20 years that chess is speeding up, so I was a bit bewildered by this surprised and indignant crowd that suddenly started screaming 'bloody murder', just as I was getting comfortable in my Chess Academy to watch a super-exciting fast-paced tiebreaker for the World Championship. As you will know by now, I personally love it that chess is getting faster and that faster players are getting the kudos for their efforts. With the help of engines and table-bases, the chess players of today should be much

better equipped to look and find strong moves faster than when I was playing chess professionally. Likewise, the addition of time increments in tournament games has certainly created the possibility of finding strong moves using the recurring 30 seconds added to your clock. In my day, 30 seconds was what six-time U.S. Champion Walter Browne would usually have left to make 20 moves or so, after spending way too much time trying to figure out some interesting quirk in an unfamiliar opening.

Solving puzzles

The introduction of excellent applications like Puzzle Rush on chess.com has shown that people that find good moves faster, either in mates in 1 or in more or less complicated studies, are on the top of the chess food chain

these days. At the time of writing this, Hikaru Nakamura is the leader in the Puzzle Push contest, having managed to solve 55 problems in five minutes, a feat that makes my mind dizzy, as I only managed 45 in over a hundred attempts.

In the Universal Chess Rating system promoted by Garry Kasparov's team, which combines activity in all time-controls, Hikaru is the second highest-rated player after Magnus Carlsen, which is a tribute to his amazing ability to play great chess fast.

Chess is getting faster and my position is that instead of fighting it, we should embrace it and get ready for it. With the much-needed facelift that FIDE recently got and the coming of a new age, I can't wait for the new market-minded team of my friends to get the show on the road and promote

'I personally love it that chess is getting faster and that faster players are getting the kudos for their efforts.'

The finalists of the 2018 chess.com speed chess championship at the Olympiad in Batumi. Before the match USA-Azerbaijan, Hikaru Nakamura was reading a book on the best summit hikes in Colorado, while Wesley So preferred a Jonathan Kellerman novel, *Motive*.

the beauty of chess, not only because of its deep concepts, but also because of its sporting element – showcased by faster time-controls – can and will attract bigger crowds and therefore more sponsors and simply a different number of zeroes for tournament prizes in the near future.

New format

As the discussion about a new format for the World Chess Championship – and hopefully also for the current regular tournaments – is taking place, I would like to throw in a suggestion to be discussed at chess coffee shops around the world. Of course, I am not the first one to offer it, but I would certainly like to second the motion. It would work like this: Every tournament game – with a somewhat faster time control than we are used to; G/60 with 30-second increments seems reasonable – should, in case of a draw, immediately be followed by a G/25 with 10-second increments and reversed colours. If that game is also drawn, a further three-minute, two-second increment game would be played, once again with reversed colours. If drawn once again, the black player in the blitz game would pick the colour

for the Armageddon game that would follow immediately.

The winner of that game would get the point for that round. The total time to bring about a result would be about the same as is needed for G/100 with 30-second increments, yet, analogous to backgammon, there would be a result that would make the spectators and the sponsors happy.

Additionally, the ratings would be applied to each speed separately, but would then be calculated as one under the Universal Rating System. The excuse that you lost because you got into time-trouble would no longer be part of the chess vocabulary, since playing good moves fast will simply be part of what makes a good chess player good.

Nakamura-So

As we prepare for this beautiful future ahead of us, let's look at some key games from the recently concluded Chess.com Blitz Championship. In the absence of Magnus Carlsen, the event was cleanly won by Hikaru Nakamura. As Hikaru had no trouble at all disposing of some of the best players in the world on his way to the final, Wesley So, who made it there by destroying the pre-match favourite Jan-Krzysztof Duda in the semis,

came well prepared. He was able to hold his own in both the 5-minute and 3-minute segments, only to lose in the bullet portion of the match.

When all is said and done, it is pretty clear that the real test of the best blitz player in the world comes down to a match between Magnus and Hikaru. I truly wish we will see an official match between these two magnificent blitz players in the near future.

To dispel the notion that blitz is too superficial and cannot generate any interesting ideas, I would like to showcase some key games from the Nakamura-So match to prove how much we can learn by looking at, and indeed studying, blitz games. We start with Game 1 of the match, in which Wesley So equalized early and showed that he is a real threat, able to unseat Hikaru from his comfortable position.

Hikaru Nakamura
Wesley So
chess.com 5m+1spm 2018 (1)
Queen's Pawn Opening

1.d4 ♘f6 2.♘f3 e6 3.e3 c5 4.♗d3 b6 5.0-0 ♗b7 6.c4 ♗e7 7.♘c3 cxd4 8.exd4 d5 9.cxd5 ♘xd5 10.♗b5+ ♗c6

11.♕a4

Hikaru Nakamura's preference for systems used at the beginning of the 20th century in blitz is admirable and nostalgic in a nice way, but this pseudo-aggressive move happens to be misplaced – just as the bishop on c6 would have been if White had played 11.♗c4! instead, continuing to fight for an opening advantage.

11...♕d7!

12.♗xc6 This excellent rejoinder is based on a pair of in-between-moves that await White if he goes for 12.♘e5?. In that case, 12...♘xc3 13.♕c2 ♕d5! 14.♗xc6+ ♘xc6 15.♘xc6 ♕xc6 would give Black a slight advantage similar to the one in the game.

12...♘xc6 13.♗e3 ♘xc3 14.bxc3 0-0 15.♖fd1 ♖fd8 16.♖ac1?!

Hikaru simply misses Black's simplification shot 16...♘e5!, but Wesley misses it as well. But only for one more move.

16...♖ac8 17.c4 ♘e5! Now Black will be slightly better in the ensuing endgame. **18.♕xd7 ♘xf3+ 19.gxf3 ♖xd7**

20.c5!
To Hikaru's credit, he always finds a way to go forward. Staying put in this position would be tantamount to resigning.

20...♖dc7

21.cxb6?
This erroneous decision was probably based on Hikaru's feeling that he would be getting in d5 at some point, with no problems in the endgame. As we will see, that will not be so easy. The a7-pawn is a target and White should have had no problem equalizing if he had aimed at it with 21.♖c3, followed shortly by ♖a3.

21...♖xc1 22.♖xc1
Hikaru's continued trust in the bishop ending is misguided. Keeping the rooks on would have been much safer.

22...♖xc1+ 23.♗xc1 axb6 24.a4
This move is necessary to fix the b6-pawn on a dark square, but now Black gets to block the d5-pawn with his king.

24...♔f8

25.♗e3?! This move looks like a serious inaccuracy, allowing Wesley to get his king to d5, thanks to the freeing of the e7-square. But even after 25.♔f1 ♔e8 26.♔e2 ♔d7 27.♔d3 ♔c6 28.♔c4 g5! White should not be able to save the game.

25...♗d8 26.♔f1 ♔e7 27.♗f4 ♔d7 28.♔e2 ♔c6 29.♔d3 ♔d5

30.♗e5 Hikaru puts on his tricking hat. Black has to decide whether it's time to move the pawn to g5. After some thought he played:

30...g6 As we will see, 30...g5 would have been fine, since it was part of a winning plan for Black.

31.h3 h5

32.♔c3 Blocking the g-pawn with 32.f4 would create too many weaknesses. A sample line could go 32...f6 33.♗b8 ♔e7 34.♔c3 h4 35.f3 ♔c6 36.♔c4 ♔b7!, trapping the bishop.

32...f6 33.♗b8 f5 33...g5! would lead to similar positions as in the game, without giving White the amazing chance to survive that we will see below.

34.♗e5 After 34.♔b4 ♗f6 35.♗c7 g5 36.♗xb6 (36.♔b5 loses to 36...g4 37.fxg4 fxg4 38.hxg4 h4 39.g5 ♗xg5 40.♔xb6 ♗f6 41.a5 ♗xd4+ 42.♔b7 e5)

ANALYSIS DIAGRAM

36...♔c6!! Black goes out to trap the bishop before breaking through on the kingside: 37.♗a7 ♗e7+ 38.♔c4 ♔b7 39.♗c5 ♗xc5 40.dxc5 h4! 41.♗d3 ♔c6!. The point! White's king is just in time to stop the h-pawn, but it is useless otherwise, and Black will clean up on the queenside before winning

the game on the other flank.
34...♗h4

35.♗c7?
With this move Hikaru misses a miraculous escape. After the active 35.♔b4!! ♔c6 36.♔c4 (or 36.♗g3 ♗e7+ 37.♔c4 h4 38.♗e5 g5) 36...♗xf2 37.♗f6! ♗e3 (37...♗g3 38.h4 ♗d6 39.♗d8) 38.h4! White sets up a fortress.
It seems that the best chance for Black in this variation is actually 35...♗xf2 36.♔b5 g5 37.♔xb6 ♗xd4+ 38.♗xd4

♔xd4 39.a5 g4 40.hxg4 fxg4 41.fxg4 hxg4 42.a6 g3 43.a7 g2 44.a8♕ g1♕ 45.♔c7!, the only move leading to a tablebase draw, since the second best one, 45.♕a5, leads to a gory, albeit anything but obvious mate in 85, according to the same tablebases.
35...♔c6 36.♗g3 ♗f6 37.♔c4 g5

38.♗e5?
It's too late to save the game, because after 38.♗b8 h4 39.♗h2 ♗e7 40.♔d3 ♗d6 41.♗g1 ♔d5 42.♔c3 f4 White would be playing without the bishop.

38...♗xe5 39.dxe5 h4 40.♔d4 g4

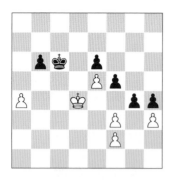

White resigned. Judging by Hikaru's facial expression, it seems that he simply miscalculated how long it would take for him to queen his g-pawn.

The next game I want to show was ultimately won by Nakamura and features a very instructive king and pawn ending. Truly, the more you know the more you don't know!

Hikaru Nakamura
Wesley So
chess.com 5m+1spm 2018 (4)
Ruy Lopez, Berlin Defence

1.e4 e5 2.♘f3 ♘c6 3.♗b5 ♘f6 4.0-0 ♘xe4 5.♖e1 ♘d6 6.♘xe5 ♗e7 7.♗f1 ♘xe5 8.♖xe5 0-0 9.♘c3 ♘e8 10.♘d5 ♗d6 11.♖e1 c6 12.♘e3 ♗e7 13.c4 ♘c7 14.d4 d5 15.cxd5 ♗b4 16.♗d2 ♗xd2 17.♕xd2 ♘xd5 18.♘xd5 ♕xd5 19.♖e5 ♕d6 20.♗c4 ♗d7 21.♖ae1 ♖ae8 22.♕c3 ♖xe5 23.dxe5 ♕e7 24.♖d1 ♗e6 25.♗xe6 ♕xe6

26.a3 The first new move, although, frankly, this position is just boring. Wesley So himself played this as White

against Fabiano Caruana, eventually drawing after 26.♕a5 b5 27.♕xa7 ♕xe5.

26...f6 27.exf6 ♕xf6 28.♕b3+ ♔h8 29.f3 b6 30.♖d7 ♖d8 31.♕f7 ♕xf7 32.♖xd8+ ♕g8 33.♖xg8+ ♔xg8 34.♔f2

This does not look like a very exciting position, since both sides have a three vs two pawn majority, so with optimum play the position should logically end in a draw. But it turned out that the best play was not so easy to find!

34...♔f7 35.♔e3 ♔e6 36.♔e4 g6 An interesting decision. It looks more natural to go for a passed pawn on the queenside with ...c5. Still, after 36...c5 37.f4 the threat of displacing the king from e6 would probably get Black to play ...g6.

37.f4 h5 38.g3 a5 Wesley is reluctant to play ...c5, so he sets a nasty trap.

39.h3? Amazingly, a losing move. White should have dealt with Black's threat of blocking two pawns with one by reacting on the queenside. After 39.b3 Black would have to wait with his king, since moving the queenside pawns would get them blocked. After 39...♔f6 40.h3 ♔e6 41.g4 hxg4 42.hxg4 ♔f6 43.f5 gxf5+ 44.gxf5

ANALYSIS DIAGRAM

Black can play 44...a4 at once to draw by force, or wait till he has withdrawn

'The real test of the best blitz player in the world comes down to a match between Magnus and Hikaru.'

his king, e.g. 44...a4 45.b4 c5 46.bxc5 bxc5 47.♔d5 ♔xf5 48.♔xc5 ♔e6, with a draw.

39...a4! 40.g4

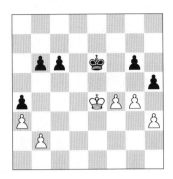

Now Black had one and only one winning move. Can you find it? Wesley did not and played the automatic:

40...hxg4?

Instead, after 40...c5! Black wins in all variations. The key is that Black will retain at least one pawn on the kingside that will queen, because White's king will try to deal with the queen-side pawns. Let's see: 41.f5+ gxf5+ 42.gxf5+ ♔f6 43.h4 b5 44.♔d5 b4! 45.♔xc5 bxa3 46.bxa3 ♔xf5 47.♔b4 ♔g4 48.♔xa4 ♔xh4 49.♔b5 ♔g5 and Black will queen first and stop White from queening.

41.hxg4

Now it's Black turn to be careful. The two drawing moves, 41...b5 to start the queenside going, and the more posi-tional 41...♔d6, are sufficient to draw for their own reasons.

41...♔f6?

But this is wrong and will lose.
He should have gone 41...b5 42.f5+ gxf5+ 43.gxf5+ ♔d6! 44.f6 ♔e6 45.♔d4 ♔d6!

ANALYSIS DIAGRAM

The key nuance. Black has to kick White's king with ...c5+ before going after the f-pawn: 46.f7 c5+ 47.♔e4 ♔e7 48.♔d5 b4! 49.♔xc5 bxa3 50.bxa3 ♔xf7, and draw.
He could also have played 41...♔d6 42.f5

ANALYSIS DIAGRAM

42...g5!!.
Surprisingly enough, allowing White a protected passed pawn is the only way to draw here, because White has no active option except to sacrifice it on f7, which happens to be insuffi-cient, because Black will trade pawns on the queenside. For example: 43.f6 ♔e6 44.f7 ♔xf7 45.♔f5 b5 46.♔xg5 c5 47.♔f5 b4 48.♔e4 bxa3 49.bxa3 ♔g6 50.♔d5 ♔g5 51.♔xc5 ♔xg4 52.♔b4 ♔f5 53.♔xa4 ♔e6 54.♔b5 ♔d7, and Black will be in time to reach the drawing c8 haven. Or 43.♔d3 c5 44.♔c3 b5 45.b3 axb3 46.♔xb3 c4+ 47.♔c3 ♔c5!, and White is stopped from separating the pawns with a4.

ANALYSIS DIAGRAM

42.♔d4?

Hikaru misses his chance. After the strongest reply, 42.f5!, Black has two options: blocking with ...g5 or going for a queen and pawn ending after capturing the pawn. Let's take a look:
– 42...g5 43.♔d4 ♔e7 44.♔c4 ♔d6 45.♔b4 b5 46.♔a5 ♔c7 47.f6 ♔d6 48.♔b6, and things are getting pretty clear.
– 42...gxf5+ is Black's only chance: 43.gxf5 c5 44.♔d5 ♔xf5 45.♔c6 ♔e4 46.♔xb6 ♔d4 47.♔b5 ♔d5 48.♔xa4 ♔c4!. An interesting endgame has arisen, but it is not completely winning for White, since Black can avoid trading pawns. 49.b4 ♔d5! 50.b5 c4 51.♔b4 ♔d4 52.b6 c3 53.b7 c2 54.b8♕ c1♕ 55.♕d6+ ♔e4, and this position is a draw according to the tablebases, although my money would be on Hikaru in a blitz game.

42...♔e6 43.♔c4 ♔d6 44.♔d4 ♔e6 45.♔e4 ♔f6? Oblivious to the problems in the position, Wesley errs again.

46.f5! gxf5+! 47.gxf5 c5 48.♔d5

♔xf5 49.♚c6 ♚e5 50.♚xb6 ♚d4
51.♚b5

51...c4?
The final mistake in this instructive endgame. Wesley misses his chance of a miraculous save with 51...♚d5!.
52.♚xa4
Now the win is elementary. Black resigned.

We'll conclude with a bullet game, because this was after all the section in which Nakamura prevailed. I believe this is the first bullet game I have ever annotated, but it's quite amazing that these two great players managed to pack so much excitement into a two-minute fist fight.

Hikaru Nakamura
Wesley So
chess.com 1m+1spm 2018 (21)
Queen's Pawn Opening, Colle System

1.♘f3 d5 2.b3 e6 3.♗b2 ♘f6 4.e3 ♗e7 5.c4 0-0 6.d4

This method of development has certainly become Hikaru's go-to opening for fast time-controls recently.
6...c5 7.dxc5 dxc4 8.♘bd2
Kind of a novelty, since only 8.♗xc4

'It's quite amazing that these two great players managed to pack so much excitement into a two-minute fist fight.'

and 8.♕xd8 have been played here before.
8...cxb3 9.♘xb3 ♘bd7 10.♖c1

10...b6?
It's hard to criticize anything that takes one second to play, but my gut reaction would be to start kicking the ground from under the b3-knight with 10...a5!.
11.c6 ♘c5
It was certainly worth throwing in 11...♗b4+ first for good measure.
12.♕xd8 ♖xd8 13.♗b5 ♘d3+ 14.♗xd3 ♖xd3 15.♘e5 ♗b4+ 16.♔e2 ♖d5 17.f3 ♗a6+ 18.♔f2 ♗d6

Remarkably enough, both sides are navigating this complicated position rather well, with White having ample compensation for the two bishops in the shape of the c6-pawn.
19.♘c4 ♗c7 20.e4 ♖d3
In bullet, good players are reluctant to withdraw their pieces, trying to stay as

active as possible. Preparing to block the c-pawn with 20...♖dd8 would have been a better choice, though.
21.♗e5 ♗xc4 22.♗xc7

22...b5?
The first real mistake of the game. Black easily blocks the pawn with ...♘e8, followed by ...♗a6, with a roughly equal game. Now ♘a5 will break the blockade.
23.♗e5 ♖c8 24.♘a5 ♖d2+ 25.♔g3 ♘h5+ 26.♔h4 f6 27.♘xc4 bxc4 28.♗c3 ♖xg2 29.♔xh5 ♖xc6

Although White is up a piece, the technical part is not so easy, since Black will be able to snipe a few pawns if he plays his rooks right.
30.♔h4 ♖c5
Wesley is looking to get in a cheap shot like ...g6 or ...♖cg5, looking for some lateral mates. Better was 30...♖a6, going for the a-pawn.

31.♖cg1 ♖xa2
31...♖cg5 was a better try, but it's a difficult decision to be made on the spot.
32.♗xf6 g6 33.♔g3 c3 34.♖a1 ♖xa1 35.♖xa1 c2 36.♖c1 a5 37.♔f2

This looks over and out. But Wesley has a few surprises up his sleeve.
37...a4 38.♗b2

38...♖h5!
A nice try for a skewer, but Hikaru avoids it.
39.♔g3 ♖c5 40.♔f4 ♔f7 41.♔e3
Hikaru walks into another trick.
41...a3 42.♗d4
Avoiding 42.♗xa3 ♖c3+.
42...♖c6 43.♔d3 a2

44.♖xc2?
Finally walking into a real trap. To avoid it, White would have had to play 44.♗a1 first.
44...♖d6!
And suddenly it's objectively a draw, because Black wins back the piece.
45.♖xa2 e5 46.♖a4

46...♔e6?
Once again trouble in endgames. Black should have set up a blockade with 46...g5!, with a drawn position.
47.♔e3?
White should have played f4 himself, with real winning chances. After 47.f4 exd4 48.♖a7 White simply wins the h-pawn, as well as, after 48...♖c6 49.♖xh7 ♖c3+ 50.♔xd4 ♖f3 51.♖h4 ♔f6 52.e5+ ♔f5 53.♖h8, the game.
47...exd4+ 48.♖xd4 ♖a6 49.♖d2 g5

50.♔f2
The best chance in this endgame is to place the pawn on h5, which can be achieved by playing 50.h4 h6 51.♖d5 ♔f6 52.h5, although it's not at all clear that White has a winning plan.
50...♖a1 51.♖d5 h6 52.h4 ♔f6 53.♖d6+ ♔g7 54.hxg5 hxg5

55.♔g3

Now the position is just a draw, and Wesley kept his cool for a while before hallucinating his way into a lost king and pawn ending in the position after move 79.
55...♖g1+ 56.♔h2 ♖f1 57.♔g2 ♖a1 58.♖c6 ♔f7 59.♔f2 ♔g7 60.♔e3 ♖a3+ 61.♔f2 ♖a1 62.♖d6 ♔f7 63.♔g2 ♔g7 64.♔h3 ♖g1 65.♖d2 ♔f6 66.♖g2 ♖f1 67.♔g4 ♔e5 68.♖g3 ♔f6 69.♖g2 ♔e5 70.♔g3 ♔f6 71.♖f2 ♖g1+ 72.♔h2 ♖a1 73.♔h3 ♔e5 74.♔g3 ♖g1+ 75.♖g2 ♖a1 76.♔g4 ♔f6 77.♔h2 ♖g1+ 78.♔h3 ♔e5 79.♖g2

79...♖xg2? 80.♔xg2 ♔f4 81.♔f2!
The only winning move and now White will win with the pawn Black had decided *not* to take.
Black resigned.

As you can see, blitz games played by strong players provide a lot of content for learning and understanding where our mistakes come from. By playing many games and analysing them we can spot typical recurring issues and work on them to become better chess players. Good Luck! ■

Not a bad time to be reading chess books

The holiday season is a time for relaxation, watching the World Rapid & Blitz, and spending a copious amount of time at the dinner table. **MATTHEW SADLER** happily gave in to the lure of fine food and drink, but didn't forget to taste a wide variety of fresh new chess books (and one DVD) too.

As I was watching Magnus Carlsen's adventures during the first two days of the World Rapid in St. Petersburg, I realized once again how nice and safe normal life is! While the best player in the world was losing his first two games and venturing 1.e4 e5 2.♕h5, work was finished for me for the year, and my most challenging puzzle was working out how many kilometres I needed to run in order to work off the calories from my mum's Christmas cooking (52, in case you're wondering!). However, since the exercise regime would have to wait until I could physically move again, it was not a bad time to be reading chess books, with a glass of port and a mince pie or two of course.

I'd like to start with the ChessBase DVD *Master Class Vol.10: Mikhail Botvinnik* by Dr. Karsten Müller, Mihail Marin, Oliver Reeh and Yannick Pelletier. I've reviewed DVDs from this series very positively over the past couple of years and this

DVD keeps up the high standard. Four authors examine different facets of Botvinnik's play: the opening is covered by Yannick Pelletier, Mihail Marin analyses the distinguishing features of Botvinnik's middlegame play, while – as always in this series – Dr. Karsten Müller takes care of the endgames and Oliver Reeh presents the best tactics. I can't think of an easier way to get a feel for the play of a great player than these DVDs: ideal training material for both young and old alike.

From my perspective, the most interesting part of the DVD is the middlegame part, which, as always, is excellently presented by Mihail Marin. Marin typifies Botvinnik's style as 'positional-aggressive': a player who conducted the game primarily according to strategical considerations but who was able to act with great power once he felt that all the necessary conditions for realising his advantage were present. 'All the necessary conditions' is the key part of that last sentence. Marin demonstrates some examples

in which Botvinnik preferred to maintain or increase his advantage by strategic means rather than exploit a tactical opportunity that seemed uncertain to him (even if the tactical solution was objectively better and even if he saw quite a few elements of the tactical solution).

Take a look at this example:

Mikhail Botvinnik
Bent Larsen
Palma de Mallorca 1967
Réti Opening

1.c4 ♘f6 2.♘f3 e6 3.g3 d5 4.♗g2 ♗e7 5.0-0 0-0 6.b3 c5 7.♗b2 ♘c6 8.e3 b6 9.♘c3 ♗b7 10.d3 ♖c8 11.♖c1 ♖c7 12.♕e2 ♖d7 13.♖fd1 ♖e8
Here Botvinnik spotted a method to change the pawn structure in his favour, exploiting Black's temporarily awkward major pieces, particularly the queen on d8 and the rook on d7.
14.cxd5 ♘xd5 14...exd5 15.♗h3 ♖c7 16.♘b5 wins the exchange.
15.♘xd5 ♖xd5 15...exd5 16.d4 leads to a pleasant hanging pawns structure for White. Larsen avoids changing the pawn structure radically, but the awkward position of the rook on d5 gives White a large number of attacking tempi.
16.d4 ♕a8 17.dxc5 Seemingly the prelude to dull exchanges, but this is anything but the case!
17...♖xd1+ 18.♖xd1 ♗xc5 19.♘g5 Threatening 20.♕h5 or 20.♕c2. **19...h6**

20.♘e4
As Marin points out, this is the first time that Botvinnik rejects a tactical

solution to the position, preferring a very strong positional idea instead.

He could have played 20.♘xf7 ♔xf7 21.♕g4 ♗f8, and now the very strong idea 22.♗e4 threatening 23.♕g6+. The key point is that Black cannot bring the knight closer to the kingside: 22...♘e7 (22...♖c8 23.♕g6+ ♔g8 24.♕h7+ ♔f7 25.♗g6+ ♔e7 26.♗xg7 and wins) 23.♕f3+ picks up the bishop on b7.

20...♗f8

21.♖d7

The second time that Botvinnik could have calculated a tactical solution to the position. However, the move played is again an extremely strong positional move, establishing the rook on the seventh rank and asking Black to take ever more desperate measures to counter White's renewed threat of 21.♘f6+.

Here the tactical solution was 21.♘f6+ gxf6 22.♕g4+ ♔h7 23.♗e4+ f5 24.♗xf5+ exf5 25.♕xf5+ ♔g8 26.♕g4+ (26.♕f6 ♘e5) 26...♔h7 27.♖d7, with the key idea 27...♘e7 28.♖xe7 ♖xe7 29.♕f5+ ♔g8 30.♕f6 ♔h7 31.g4 followed by 32.♕h8+ and 33.♕g8 mate.

21...f5 22.♘d6 ♗xd6

23.♖xd6

Marin shows that this is the third moment that Botvinnik eschews a tactical win, preferring a simple positional move that increases White's control over the dark squares.

23.♖xg7+ ♔f8 24.♖h7 was the win that Botvinnik found after the game – 25.♕h5 is threatened and Black cannot defend the seventh rank with 24...♖e7, due to 25.♖h8+.

23...♘d4 24.♖xd4 ♗xg2 25.♖d7 ♗h3 As Marin shows, 25...♗h1 would have given Black some (shaky) chances to grovel on after 26.f4 (26. f3 ♕xf3 27.♖xg7+ ♔f8 28.♕d2 e5 29.♖xa7 ♕c6 is, amazingly, still not over for Black!) 26...e5 27.♗xe5 ♖c8 28.♖xg7+ ♔f8 29.♘c7 ♖xc7 30.♗xc7 ♕d5. This is not easy for White to win, as Marin points out.

26.f3 ♖d8 27.♖xg7+ ♔f8 28.♖h7

Master Class Vol.10:
Mikhail Botvinnik
Müller, Marin, Reeh,
Pelletier
FritzTrainer DVD
ChessBase 2018
★★★★☆

but each successive strong positional move that Botvinnik played (20.♘e4, 21.♖d7, 22.♘d6 and 23.♖xd6) forced an additional weakness and made Black's position look increasingly cheerless.

Although it may not be enough to defeat a defensive monster like an engine, from a human point of view Botvinnik's restrained play was just as difficult to defend against as a direct attack, and the impression

---

'Botvinnik was able to act with great power once he felt that all the necessary conditions for realising his advantage were present.'

♕d5 29.♔f2 ♕d1 30.♖h8+ ♔f7 31.♖xd8 ♕xd8 32.♕c2 ♕d5 33.♕c7+ ♔e8 34.♕b8+ ♔d7 35.♕xa7+ ♔c8 36.♕a6+ ♔c7 37.♕c4+ ♕xc4 38.bxc4 ♔c6 39.♗d4 h5 40.a4 ♔c7 41.c5 bxc5 42.♗xc5 ♔c6 43.♗b4 ♔b6 44.g4 hxg4 45.♔g3 e5 46.e4 fxe4 47.fxg4
Black resigned.

I found this interesting and spent some time thinking about it. Botvinnik aimed for positions in which he stood well strategically: he controlled the centre, his pieces were more active, the opponent's pieces were misplaced. From this basis, there are many good types of moves in the realisation of the advantage: not only tactical ones, but also positional ones. It's tempting just to focus on the missed tactical wins,

we have of the game is that a strong player as Larsen was squeezed off the board by very simple means. Bear in mind also that Botvinnik's continued strong positional play gave him multiple chances of finishing off the game tactically due to the difficulties Larsen experienced in defending the position. A very interesting and entertaining DVD!

■ ■ ■

Hot on the heels of the fantastic first volume of the biography of Emanuel Lasker by Forster, Negele and Tischbierek (reviewed in New In Chess 2018/8) comes *Lasker – Move by Move* by Zenon Franco (Everyman). The book follows the standard Everyman pattern for the Move by Move series: 46 complete games are presented, with most of the moves receiving at least a brief comment. The emphasis

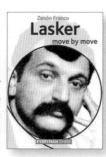

**Lasker
Move by Move
Zenon Franco
Everyman 2018**
★★★★☆

**Queen's Gambit
Declined: Vienna
Ilczuk & Panczyk
Everyman 2018**
★★★☆☆

is on explanations rather than long variations, and there are frequent interjections from a fictive reader, asking common-sense questions when the game (or the explanation) gets too complicated. The typeface is large and there are a copious number of diagrams, which makes the book easy to read.

It's a well-worked out concept and I've again enjoyed a number of books from this series. I also enjoyed this one a lot. A well-written introduction starts us off by giving an overview of Lasker's style and his play in each phase of the game. The book then proceeds chronologically through Lasker's career, mixing well-known and less famous games.

One fine game that had completely escaped my notice was Lasker's win against Frank Marshall in New York 1924. Because of Lasker's phenomenal career score against Marshall (Marshall won their first encounter in 1900, but had to wait until 1940 – in which time

Lasker had notched up 12 wins – for his next in a mini-match played a year before Lasker's death in 1941!) I guess I always tend to shrug my shoulders when I see one of their games, but looking through a few games I wonder whether I need to revise my opinion. Maybe it's just that Marshall brought out the best in Lasker! In any case, this was a game played with great imagination by both players!

**Emanuel Lasker
Frank Marshall**
New York 1924
Ruy Lopez, Exchange Variation

1.e4 e5 2.♘f3 ♘c6 3.♗b5 a6 4.♗xc6 dxc6 5.d4 ♗g4

A typically ingenious Marshall Gambit that hasn't been repeated by any strong player since.

6.dxe5 ♛xd1+ 7.♔xd1 0-0-0+ 8.♔e1 ♗c5 9.h3 ♗h5 10.♗f4 f5

A great move, shaking up White's pawn structure!

11.♘bd2 11.exf5 ♗xf3 12.gxf3 ♖f8 gives Black reasonable compensation for the pawn.

11...♘e7 12.♗g5 ♗xf3 13.gxf3 ♖he8 14.♖d1 fxe4 15.fxe4 h6 16.♗h4 ♗d4 17.♘c4 g5

17...b5 18.c3 was Lasker's idea.

18.c3 ♘g6 19.cxd4 ♘xh4 20.♔e2 ♖d7

20...♖f8, preventing White's next move and threatening either 21...♖f4, 21...♖f3 or 21...♘f3, was Black's only way to keep life in the position. Once White consolidates with f2-f3, Black is really struggling.

21.f3 ♘g6 21...♖ed8 doesn't carry a threat as Franco points out. If 22.♖hf1 ♖xd4, 23.♘d6+ wins the exchange.

22.♘e3 c5 23.dxc5 ♘f4+ 24.♔f2 ♖xd1 25.♖xd1 ♖xe5 26.♘d5 ♘xh3+ 27.♔g3 g4 28.♘f6 h5

29.f4 ♖xc5 30.♖e1

Really nice technique: the knight on f6 both keeps the black king at bay and attacks Black's kingside pawns, while the rook supports the advance of the e-pawn. Black's pieces are active but uncoordinated and his position now collapses.

30...♖b5 31.e5 ♔d8 32.♘xh5 ♔e7 33.f5 ♘g5 34.♔xg4 ♘h7 35.♘f4 ♖xb2 36.♘d5+ ♔d7 37.e6+ ♔d6 38.e7 ♔xd5 39.♖e6 ♖g2+ 40.♔f4 ♖g8 41.e8♕ ♖xe8 42.♖xe8 c5 43.♖d8+ ♔c6 44.♖h8 And that was win number 11 for Lasker! A really nice book!

■ ■ ■

Queen's Gambit Declined: Vienna by Ilczuk & Panczyk (Everyman) is a book that I've been meaning to read for quite a while, but I only got around to it a couple of weeks ago. The book is a detailed examination of the variations arising from this position:

Writing this, we touch straight-away on the greatest shortcoming of this book, namely move orders. As you can imagine, this position can

Test Your Chess Skills
Sarhan & Logman
Guliev
New In Chess 2018
★★★★☆

be reached via different paths. The move order specified on the back of the book – 1.d4 d5 2.c4 e6 3.♘c3 ♘f6 4.♘f3 ♗b4 5.♗g5 dxc4 – is slightly off for two reasons:

1. If you play the QGD via this move order, you will likely never see the Vienna, as White is most likely to

play 4.cxd5 and transpose into an Exchange QGD (3...♗e7 is common at top level to avoid this).

2. 4...♗b4 leads to a Ragozin, against which 5.♗g5 is just one of many moves (5.♕a4+ and 5.cxd5 are major alternatives). You'd be much more likely to get the positions covered in this book if you played 4...dxc4, after which 5.e4 ♗b4 6.♗g5 is the main way of playing.

More confusingly still, the intro-duction gives the move order 1.d4 d5 2.c4 e6 3.♘c3 ♘f6 4.♘f3 dxc4 5.♗g5 ♗b4, the illustrative games throughout the book use all sorts of move orders, while the introduc-tory moves for each chapter vary between the 4...♗b4 move order (Chapter 1) and 4...dxc4 (Chapter 2). I understand that this is not a pure repertory book, and more an exami-nation of one specific variation, but I think it's important to know how best to reach the line, what the pros and cons are and what the likelihood is of reaching your main lines. That's especially important when you consider the difficult nature of the

Chess Calculation Training Volume 3: Legendary Games
Romain Edouard
Thinkers Publishing
2018
★★★☆☆

positions that Black must face in the main lines in this opening. I haven't made an exact count, but it seems to me that a significant propor-tion of the illustrative games end in White wins and I think Black players would have to invest a significant amount of work to remember a few

'Putting my doubts to one side, I started to solve some of the positions and found I enjoyed it quite a lot.'

critical paths through the opening minefield!

This criticism aside, the book is generally well-structured and well-researched (although I did have the feeling that Richard Pert's excellent Quality Chess book on the Ragozin, which advocates transposing to a Vienna after 4...♗b4 5.♗g5 dxc4, had not been taken account of) and is a useful reference for any Black player brave enough to take up this variation!

■ ■ ■

Test Your Chess Skills by the Guliev brothers Sarhan and Logman (New In Chess) is a puzzle book with a difference. 224 exercises are presented, and for most of the posi-tions the reader is asked whether the side to move is (for example) A: Hopeless, B: Winning, C: Equal, and then asked to justify his opinion with a variation.

I wasn't quite sure what to make of it at first, but putting my doubts to one side, I started to solve some of the positions and found I enjoyed it quite

**The Schliemann
Defence
Move by Move
Junior Tay
Everyman 2018**
★★★★☆

a lot. Some of the positions have direct tactical solutions, others require positional judgement, and some require a bit of both! The nice thing about the format is that it forces you to get your initial feelings about the position clear in your head instead of heading straight into a search for a direct solution (as is the tendency in normal puzzle books), which is a good thing to learn. I'd like to give this between 3 and 4 stars, but with the spirit of Christmas still flowing through me, I'll give it 4 stars!

■ ■ ■

Chess Calculation Training – Volume 3: Legendary Games by Romain Edouard (Thinkers Publishing) is a similar effort: a puzzle book with a twist, as are most works by Thinkers Publishing! Most of the 480 exercises in this puzzle book were played before the year 2000 and many are by big-name players such as Karpov, Kramnik, Kasparov and Fischer. As always with Thinkers Publishing puzzle books, the exercises are organised into themed chapters, with sometimes surprising titles such as 'Nasty Surprises' or 'Crush your Opponent'!

I suppose the danger of choosing legendary games is that many of the exercises may be familiar to experienced puzzle solvers, and much of the material was known to me, although I must confess that knowing that I have seen the position before is never a guarantee of remembering the solution. A great example of this is the fantastic game Jussupow-Kasparov, Linares 1990.

Jussupow-Kasparov
Linares 1990
position after 38...b4

39.♕a4 Even knowing this position and having a conviction that ...c4-c3 at some point was the solution, it still took me a few minutes to work out the wonderful point!

39...c3 40.♕xe8 Kasparov won this game after 40.♖xc3 ♗d7 41.♖c4 ♗xa4 42.♖xd4 ♖b8 43.♗f1 ♗c2 44.♗c4 b3 45.♗xb3 ♖xb3 (0-1, 63).

40...♕d7 is the amazing idea, forcing the exchange of queens after which the passed pawns will queen! Astonishing!

All-in-all, a fun puzzle book.

■ ■ ■

We conclude with the excellent *The Schliemann Defence – Move by Move* by Junior Tay (Everyman). I don't know a great deal about this opening, although I have always been surprised at how tricky it is to gain an advantage when playing the main lines against it as White. Despite that I read this book with great pleasure and interest.

Tay is an excellent guide through the labyrinth of fourth move possibilities for White, explaining the nature of each approach very clearly for White: which move aims for a quiet edge, which move can lead to complications. Tay also takes an objective view of the Black side, explaining the drawbacks to certain previously attractive lines and providing detailed but still comprehensible guidance through current best practice. It's maybe nice to mention that AlphaZero also had a little go at

boosting the Black side in one of the lines Tay considers most testing:

**Stockfish 8
AlphaZero**
Computer Match London 2018
Ruy Lopez, Schliemann Defence

1.e4 e5 2.♘f3 ♘c6 3.♗b5 f5 4.♘c3 fxe4 5.♘xe4 ♘f6 6.♘xf6+ ♕xf6 7.♕e2 ♗e7 8.♗xc6 bxc6 9.♘xe5

9...♗b7 Amazingly enough, a novelty from AlphaZero: 9...0-0 and 9...♕e6 (Tay's recommendation) have been played almost exclusively. Combined with AlphaZero's trademark queenside castling and March of the Rook's Pawn towards the opponent's king, it seems like a pretty interesting way to play!

10.0-0 0-0-0 11.d3 ♖de8 12.♘c4 h5 13.♕e3 h4

Ignoring the threat against a7.

14.♕h3 ♔b8 15.♗d2 d5 16.♘c3 d4 17.♗d2 ♗c8 18.♕f3 ♕xf3 19.gxf3 ♗e6

AlphaZero gave itself a 45% expected score for Black in this position. Although Stockfish pressed, White never really got anywhere close to a serious advantage.

20.f4 h3 21.♘e5 ♗f6 22.♘xc6+ ♔c8 23.♖fe1 ♗d5 24.♖xe8+ ♖xe8 25.♘e5 ♗xe5 26.♖e1 ♔d7 27.fxe5 ♖e6 28.c4 dxc3 29.♗xc3 ♖g6+ 30.♔f1 ♗xa2 31.♖e3 ♗e6 32.♖g3 ♖xg3 33.fxg3 ♗g4

And the game was drawn in 106 moves.

A really good opening guide and a must-read for any Schliemann addicts out there! ■

'There is something about nearly every opening one can think of.'

British Chess Magazine

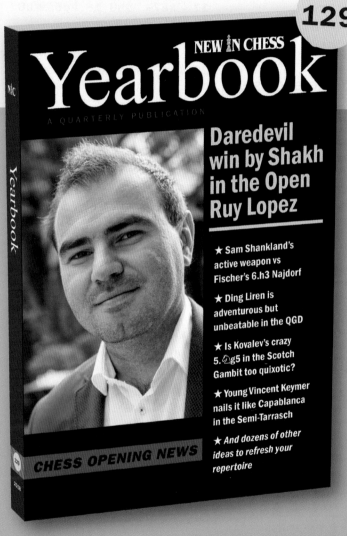

129

NEW IN CHESS

Yearbook

A QUARTERLY PUBLICATION

Daredevil win by Shakh in the Open Ruy Lopez

★ Sam Shankland's active weapon vs Fischer's 6.h3 Najdorf

★ Ding Liren is adventurous but unbeatable in the QGD

★ Is Kovalev's crazy 5.♘g5 in the Scotch Gambit too quixotic?

★ Young Vincent Keymer nails it like Capablanca in the Semi-Tarrasch

★ And dozens of other ideas to refresh your repertoire

CHESS OPENING NEWS

paperback | 256 pages | € 29.95

With answers to urgent questions such as:

- How does Ding Liren turn a quiet QGD into a swift attack on the black king?
- Which pet KID line did Adhiban use to win a crucial Olympiad game?
- Has the Dzindzhi Opening been refuted by a French amateur?
- Is the direct 3...d5 playable after all against the Bishop's Opening?
- How does the Berlin Defence fare in correspondence chess?
- Is Kortchnoi's 10...g6 in the Open Ruy Lopez due for rehabilitation?
- How does Karjakin treat the most complicated variation of the QGD?
- Is the Bukavshin Variation of the Catalan refuted by Gelfand's 8.♘fd2?
- Does the Bayonet charge with 10.c4 ♘f4 11.a4 mean the end of the Mar del Plata KID?
- How does MVL find activity for Black in the Symmetrical English?
- What is the currently best book for studying the famous Carlsbad structure?
- What old Ruy Lopez line did Mamedyarov use to successfully confound Aronian?
- Where does Aronian put his queen's bishop in the QGD with 4...a6 ?
- Is Kovalev's crazy 5.♘g5 in the Scotch Gambit too quixotic?
- What is top talent Vincent Keymer's favourite reaction to 1.d4 ?
- What does Giuoco Piano expert Ivan Saric think of Karjakin's 5.♘c3 ?
- How does Sam Shankland react to Fischer's 6.h3 Najdorf?
- How can Black play the Four Knights Sicilian and avoid the Sveshnikov?

Jan Timman

Inspired studies

Endgame studies are not only relevant because they are often based on actual games, they also have a strong aesthetic appeal. **JAN TIMMAN** takes a look at *Practical Chess Beauty*, the book that endgame-study composer Yochanan Afek wrote about his lifelong passion.

In the world of endgame studies, the grandmaster title is not subject to inflation. There are only nineteen living grandmasters in the world, compared to over 1600 over-the-board grandmasters. One of this select company is Yochanan Afek, who was awarded the title in 2015. The 66-year-old Israeli, a long-time Amsterdam resident, is indefatigably involved in many disciplines of the game. He is a player, trainer, organizer, writer and, above all, endgame-study composer. A curious fact is that he got a Dutch residence permit because he is a composer. The authorities must have thought that composing endgame studies is something akin to composing music.

Afek recently collected his studies in *Practical Chess Beauty*. It is a lengthy work full of ideas and beauty. Having started at a young age, Afek has been composing endgame studies for no

less than half a century. I was familiar with many of his studies via Harold van der Heijden's database, but it is good to see them back with insightful commentary. Afek has arranged his studies by theme, and has added some games and fragments. His games contain many things of interest, as witness the following example.

Afek-Birnboim
Rishon-Le-Ziyyon 1992
position after 14...0-0

It's a quiet position, and it doesn't look at all as if pandemonium is about to break loose, although it must be said that this was mainly Birnboim's doing.

15.♘e5 ♗xe2 16.♘xc6 ♕b5
Looking for adventure. After 16...♕xc6 17.♕xe2 ♕d5 Black would simply have been fine.

17.♘xe7+ ♔h8 18.♖c5 ♕a6
19.♕b1 Threatening mate in two.
19...♗d3! A necessary intermediate move to maintain the balance.
20.♕c1 ♗xf1 21.♗h6! An attractive move that threatens mate again.

21...f6? Black understandably wants to keep the queen from g5, but now the seventh rank is fatally weakened. His bishop should have been dispatched to d3, with an equal position, as witness the following spectacular variation: 21...♗d3 22.♕g5 ♗g6 23.♘e5 f6 24.♘xg6+ hxg6 25.♕e4 f5 26.♕e5 ♖f7

ANALYSIS DIAGRAM

27.♗xg7+! ♖xg7 28.♖c7 ♖ag8 29.♕f6 ♕e2 30.g4! ♕e1+ 31.♔g2 ♕e4+ 32.♔g1, and Black is forced to go for a draw with perpetual check.

Yochanan Afek presented Jan Timman with a copy of his book
Practical Chess Beauty at a league match of their team of SV Wageningen.

KEES STAP

26...♖g8+ 27.♔h2 ♕d6+ 28.f4
It looks as if Black might as well resign, but...

28...♖g2+! A miraculous escape.
**29.♔xg2 ♕d5+ 30.♔h2 ♕xf7
31.♕h4 ♕e6 32.♕f2 ♕e4
33.♕d2 ♔g7 34.♔g3 ♔f7
35.♕c3 ♔e6 36.b4 ♔f7 37.a4 a6
38.b5 axb5 39.axb5 ♔g6 40.b6
♕b1 41.♕e3** Draw.

I have noticed that a number of Afek's best studies failed to win the highest distinction in endgame tournaments, but the following study was given first prize in a competition organized by the Koninklijke Schaakfederatie Antwerpens Handel (the Royal Chess Federation of Antwerp's Trade).

Afek 1997
White to play and win

There are only seven pieces on the board; it's a miniature. Otherwise, the position is quite natural, and despite the limited number of pieces it turns out to contain a multitude of hidden finesses.
1.♗f7
To prepare for queening. The bishop

22.♖c7! Afek pounces at once. White has a decisive attack.
22...♖f7

23.♘f5 The most elegant move, which shows the hand of the endgame-study composer. 23.♘g6+ hxg6 24.♖xf7 ♕c4 25.♕e3 would have been equally crushing.
23...exf5 24.♖xf7 ♗xg2 25.♔xg2
White could have won with 25.♖xg7 ♗xh3 26.♕e3, since the counter-

attack with 26...♕f1+ 27.♔h2 ♗g4 won't amount to anything, and White decides the issue with 28.♖e7. Afek goes for a different winning attempt, but one that falls just short.
25...gxh6

26.♕xh6
Still thinking that Black is on the ropes. With 26.♕c7 ♕c6+ 27.♕xc6 bxc6 28.♖xf6 White could have liquidated to a winning rook ending.

'There are only 19 living grandmasters in the world, compared to over 1600 over-the-board grandmasters.'

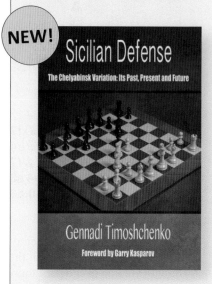
is controlling the crucial squares c4 and e8.

1...♖e5! Subtle defending. White cannot queen the pawn in view of a check on c5, followed by a family check. **2.♗c4+!** With this intermediate check White closes the c-file.

2...♘d3+! Sacrifices and counter-sacrifices. Black is going for stalemate.

3.♗xd3+ ♔e1

4.c8♖! White has to go for a minor promotion. 4.c8♕ ♖c5+ leads to stalemate. **4...♖h5 5.♖f8** Suddenly, White threatens mate. **5...♖c5+ 6.♔b2 ♖h5 7.♔c3** The mating net is tightened. On 7...♖c5+, 8.♗c4 is the simplest win.

Afek also gives fragments from other people's games if they had served as inspiration for a study. In the World Championship match of 2008, Anand won the fifth match game with a *petite combinaison*.

Kramnik-Anand
Bonn World Championship 2008 (5)
position after 33.♖xb7

Anand decided the issue with:
33...♖c1+ 34.♗f1 ♘e3! 35.fxe3 fxe3 and White resigned. The passed e-pawn is unstoppable.

Afek used this fragment to compose the following beautiful study:

Afek
2nd Prize Schach 2008
White to play and win

It is interesting to see what a good endgame composer does with such a position. The starting position is in fact a stylized version of Kramnik-Anand. **1.♘d6!** Of course. After 1.♘d4 ♖e4 White will no longer be able to win. **1...cxd6 2.cxd6 ♖e1+ 3.♔c2! ♖e2+ 4.♔c3**

White's king must stick to the c-file.

4...♖e3+ 5.♔c4 ♖e4+

6.♔c5! Not 6.♔d5?, in view of 6...♖e1 7.h5 ♖d1+, and Black can draw, e.g. 8.♔c5 ♖c1+ 9.♔d4 ♖d1+ 10.♔e5 ♖e1+ 11.♔f6 ♖d1 12.♖d8 ♔b7, and White's passed pawns are not dangerous enough.

6...♖e5+ 7.♔c6 ♖e6

The white king and the black rook have been shadowing each other step by step in a way that, in endgame-study jargon, is called 'a systematic manoeuvre'. Black has survived for the moment, but with accurate play White manages to introduce a deadly mutual zugzwang.

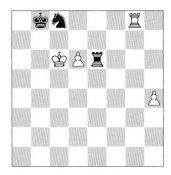

8.♖d8 ♖f6! The best defence. After 8...♖h6 9.h5! Black would be in zugzwang, e.g. 9...♖f6 10.♔c5 ♖f5+ 11.♔d4 ♔b7 12.d7 and wins.

9.♔c5! Certainly not 9.h5?, in view of 9...♖h6!, and now White is in zugzwang. 9.♔d5? was equally insufficient in view of 9...♔b7 10.♔e5 ♖h6! 11.d7 ♘d6! 12.♖f8! ♘f7+! 13.♖xf7 ♔c7, with a theoretically drawn position.

'Carlsen's lack of ambition in the classical games remains strange.'

9...♖f5+ 10.♔d4 Again, White must find the correct square for the king. After 10.♔b4? ♔b7 11.d7 ♘e7! 12.♖b8+ ♔a7 13.♖a8+ ♔b7! Black will save himself.
10...♔b7 11.d7 ♘e7

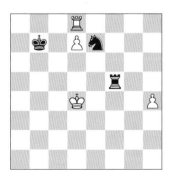

12.♖b8+! Another important finesse.
12...♔a7 13.♔e4 And wins.

In the recent Carlsen-Caruana match in London, a position arose that could be regarded as an endgame study. It

happened in Game 6, in which Caruana overlooked a complicated win.

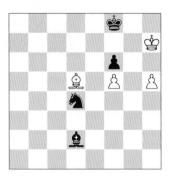

Carlsen-Caruana
London World Championship 2018 (6)
position after 66...♘d4

Carlsen had sacrificed a piece in the belief that he had a fortress. It's true that the position is drawn, but White needs to continue to play accurately.
67.♔g6? A serious mistake that could have cost White the game. There was no reason to cover the f-pawn. With 67.♗c4 ♗c3 68.♗d3 could have retained his fortress.
67...♗g5 68.♗c4

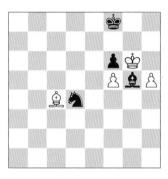

The critical moment. Caruana now played **68...♘f3**, and 11 moves later he decide to settle for a draw.
Before I show you the hidden win, I have two things to say about this fragment:
1. It is commonly thought that all classical games in the match were drawn because both players' level of chess was so high. But in 4 of the 12 games, the balance decisively shifted at one or more points. This is a relatively high percentage. There could have been four decided games – two wins each – but the player's lack of resolve put paid to that.

2. This lack of resolve must have had a psychological reason. When Petrosian unexpectedly got a winning position against Spassky in their first match game in 1966, his heart rate accelerated worryingly – the sensation of being so close to victory threatened to overwhelm him. This time, curiously enough, there were three games in which neither player realized that he was winning. I am not talking about the first game; there, it was more than obvious that Carlsen threw away a winning position due to nerves. But the final game was different. The World Champion himself said that he had underestimated his chances. His surprising draw offer in a superior position was kind of justified by his resounding victory in the rapid tiebreaks. But Carlsen's lack of ambition in the classical games remains strange. Even Petrosian, the most peace-loving of World Champions, would have gone for a win from that position in Game 12. Caruana, I thought, sometimes evinced a clear lack of motivation and confidence. In Game 8, he had outplayed his great opponent in the middlegame without fully realizing it, while in the endgame I am talking about here, he could have played on till move 114, regardless of whether it was a draw. In a World Championship match, you should go all out.

But it is understandable that he failed to see the study-like win in the diagrammed position. It would have gone as follows:
68...♗h4! 69.♗d5 ♘e2 70.♗f3

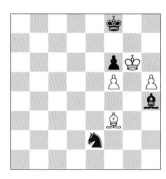

ANALYSIS DIAGRAM

and now the surprising 70...♘g1! is the key move. Black allows the white bishop

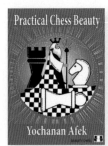

Practical Chess Beauty
by Yochanan Afek
Quality Chess 2018
hardcover 464 pages

to lock in his knight in order to land White in zugzwang, because White will be unable to keep the knight locked in indefinitely. He can try two bishop moves:

– 71.♗g4 ♔g8 72.♔h6 ♗g3 73.♔g6 ♗e5 74.♔h6 ♗f4+ 75.♔g6 ♗g5, and White is in zugzwang.

After 76.h6 ♔h8 77.h7 ♗h4 78.♔h5 ♗e1 79.♔g6 ♗c3 80.♔h6 ♗d2+ 81.♔g6 ♗g5 he will be out-manoeuvred.

– 71.♗d5 ♗g5 72.♔h7 ♘e2, and White cannot keep his bishop on the a2-g8 diagonal.

After 73.♗f3 ♘g3 74.♗g4 ♔f7 75.♔h8 ♗e3 76.♔h7 ♗d4 77.♔h8 ♗c5 78.♔h7 ♗e7 79.♔h8 ♗f8 80.♔h7 ♘e4 he will be mated. Or 73.♗c4 ♘f4 74.h6 ♘g2 75.♔g6 ♘h4+, and Black wins.

It would have been a sensation, of course, if Caruana had found this over the board. As Kasparov observed on Twitter: '... they would have requested metal detectors immediately! No human would willingly trap his own knight like that.'

In the world of endgame studies, however, there is nothing special

to letting your knight meander like this. It reminded me of one of my own recent studies, which won first honourable mention in the Dvoretsky Memorial Tournament.

Timman 2017
White to play and draw

The study is based on the final stage of the game Damaso-Navara, Jerusalem 2015. White has to sacrifice his b-pawn, because Black is threatening to take his king to c5.

1.b6! cxb6 2.♔c2

Forced, because after 2.♘d3 ♔c4, the knight would be unable to find good squares. But even after the text it remains hard to find squares for the knight.

There are two main variations now:

Variation I: 2...♗c4 3.♘d1!

Not 3.♘a4, in view of 3...b5 4.♘b6+ ♔c6 5.♘c8 ♗e6 6.♘e7+ ♔d6, and

the knight has been locked in because square g6 is inaccessible.

3...♔d4 4.♘f2 ♗e6

5.♘h1! The only move. The knight must go to g3. On 5.♘d1 b5, White is out-manoeuvred. **5...♔e3 6.♘g3 ♔f3 7.♘f1** Or 7.♘h5, and the knight is safe.

Variation II: 2...♔d4 3.♘a4!

Again, the knight has to jump to unlikely squares. After 3.♘d1 ♗e6! 4.♘f2 ♔e3 White's situation is hopeless. **3...b5 4.♘b6 ♗e6**

5.♘a8! Heading for c7.
5...♔c5 6.♘c7 ♗f7 7.♘a6+

And White saves himself. It is interesting that White needs two corner squares to take his knight to safety. ■

MAXIMize your Tactics **Solutions**

1. Santarius-Daggupati
St. Louis 2018

35...♘d4! 36.♖b4 36.♖c5 loses identically. **36...♖xh3+!** White resigned in view of 37.♔g1 ♘e2+ or 37.gxh3 ♘f3 followed by ...♖h2 mate.

2. Haug-Gholami
Porto Carras 2018

22.♖xf5! ♗xf5 22...exf5 23.♗e5+ ♕g7 24.♕e3!. **23.♗e5+ ♕xe5** Or 23...♔g8 24.♕xf5. **24.dxe5** And White went on to win.

3. Amin-Kozul
Zagreb 2018

37.d6 ♖c5 38.♘d7! 38.dxe7 ♖xe5 or 38.♘d3 ♔xh6 39.♘xc5 ♗xd6 don't work. **38...♖c8 39.dxe7 ♔xh6 40.♘f6!** And White converted.

4. Kovchan-Korobov
Kiev 2018

36.♘xd5! exd5 37.♕xh6+! With the point that after 37...gxh6 38.♖g8+ ♔h7 White now has 39.♗f5 mate. Black resigned. After 37...♔g8 38.♖xg7+ ♔xg7 39.♗e6+! ♔f8 40.♕h8+ he is checkmated as well.

5. Ter Sahakyan-Kravtsiv
Ahmedabad 2018

53...♖h1+! 54.♔xh1 ♘xg3+! 54...♘xf2+ 55.♔g1 ♕xg3+ 56.♔f1 ♖f8 (56...♕g2+? 57.♔e1 ♕g1+ 58.♗f1) 57.♖g6+ ♕xg6 58.♕xg6+ ♔xg6 59.♔xf2 is a draw. **55.fxg3 ♖h8+** And White resigned.

6. Nitin-Lalith
Xingtai 2018

25...♘xa2! 26.♔xa2 ♕c3! The threat is 27...♕b2+!, 28...axb2+ 29...♗c3+ and mate. **27.♕d2 ♕b2+! 28.♗xb2 axb2+ 29.♔xb2 ♗xd2 30.b4** Or 30.♖b1 ♗a6, 31...♗c3+ and 32...♖fa8. **30...♖a4** White resigned.

7. Nepomniachtchi-Rakhmanov
Russia 2018

34.♗xb7! ♘xb7 35.♖e4+ ♔f8 36.♖h1! White's attack is decisive. **36...f6 37.gxf6 ♖e8 38.♖h8+ ♔f7 39.♖h7+ ♔f8** And now, **40.♖eh4!** (instead of the game move 40.♖xe8+) would have mated by 41.♖g7 and 42.♖h8.

8. Kravtsiv-Gusain
Taleigao 2018

22.♗b5! ♖ac8 22...cxb5 23.♘b3+ ♔c4 24.♖e4 mate or 22...♔xd4 23.♖d1+ ♔c5 24.♗xc6 mate. **23.♗xc6** Black's position is hopeless after 23...♔xd4 24.♖d1+ or 23...♔f8 24.♘b3+ ♔b6 25.♗xd5+ ♘xe6 26.♗xe6 so he resigned.

9. Saduakassova-Matnadze
Khanty-Mansiysk 2018

Instead of 34...♖a8 35.♖e5 ♕da5 36.♖xa5 ♕xa5 37.♕xb3, **34...♖a5!** was better, threatening 35...♖a1+! 36.♔xa1 ♕a5+ with mate: **35.♖e5 ♕xd3+ 36.♖xd3 ♖a1+! 37.♔xa1 ♖c1** mate, and 35.d5 loses to 35...♖ca8 36.♔c1 ♖xd5! 37.♕xd5 ♖a1+.

Kateryna Lagno

CURRENT ELO: 2560

DATE OF BIRTH: December 27, 1989

PLACE OF BIRTH: Lvov, Ukraine

PLACE OF RESIDENCE: Moscow, Russia

What is your favourite city?
Moscow.

What was the last great meal you had?
I like Japanese and Indian food a lot, but unfortunately my favourite Indian restaurant in Moscow was recently closed.

What drink brings a smile to your face?
Cider.

Which book would you give to a dear friend?
One Flew over the Cuckoo's Nest by Ken Kesey.

What book is currently on your bedside table?
Notre-Dame de Paris by Victor Hugo.

What is your all-time favourite movie?
The Barber of Siberia directed by Nikita Mikhalkov.

And your favourite TV series?
Breaking Bad.

Do you have a favourite actor?
Oleg Menshikov.

And a favourite actress?
Kate Winslet.

What music do you listen to?
Depends on my mood, but I have never understood jazz.

Is there a work of art that moves you?
Unfortunately, I understand nothing in art.

Who is your favourite chess player?
Garry Kasparov, for his aggressive type of play.

Is there a chess book that had a profound influence on you?
Alexander Alekhine's *300 Games*.

What was your best result ever?
Winning the World Rapid Championship in 2014, the most difficult tournament I have ever played.

And the best game you played?
Vs Hou Yifan at the Tromsø Olympiad.

What is your favourite square?
As a Grünfeld and King's Indian player definitely g7.

Do chess players have typical shortcomings?
We love to complain.

What are chess players particularly good at (except for chess)?
Counting money ☺.

Do you have any superstitions concerning chess?
No.

Facebook, Instagram, Snapchat, or?
Live communication ☺.

How many friends do you have on Facebook?
I do not have Facebook.

Who do you follow on Twitter?
No one.

What is your life motto?
Look forward.

When were you happiest?
When my two-year-old son hugged me and said 'Mama is mine' ☺.

When was the last time you cried?
After losing the tie-break against Ju Wenjun at the 2018 World Championship in Khanty-Mansiysk.

Who or what would you like to be if you weren't yourself?
A singer.

Which three people would you like to invite for dinner?
Only one, my husband [Alexander Grischuk – ed.]

What is the best piece of advice you were ever given?
To read as many books as possible.

Is there something you'd love to learn?
Chinese.

What is your greatest fear?
Well, what I can say is that I am not fond of insects.

And your greatest regret?
It is a secret, but it has nothing to do with chess.

How do you relax?
Sleeping, chatting with friends.

What does it mean to be a chess player?
Nothing special.

Is a knowledge of chess useful in everyday life?
Not really.

What is the best thing that was ever said about chess?
'Nobody ever won a chess game by resigning.' – Savielly Tartakower.